SRA
Reading Mastery
Signature Edition

Language Arts Workbook

Siegfried Engelmann
Karen Lou Seitz Davis
Jerry Silbert

Columbus, OH

READING MASTERY® is a registered trademark of The McGraw-Hill Companies, Inc.

SRAonline.com

 SRA

Send all inquiries to this address:
SRA/McGraw-Hill
4400 Easton Commons
Columbus, OH 43219

ISBN: 978-0-07-612567-8
MHID: 0-07-612567-X

10 HES 13 12

The *McGraw·Hill* Companies

A

B

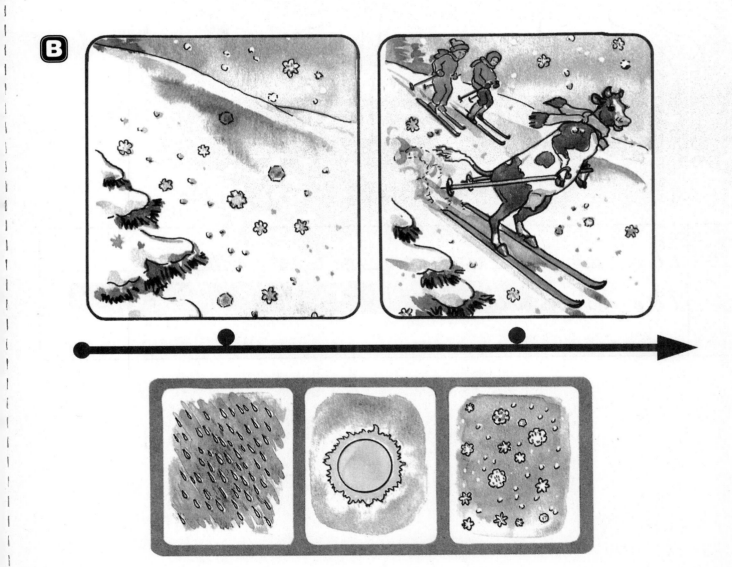

	The cat was sitting in the grass.
	The dog ████████████████████████████.

A

	The dog was sitting on the floor.
	The cat ████████████████████████ .

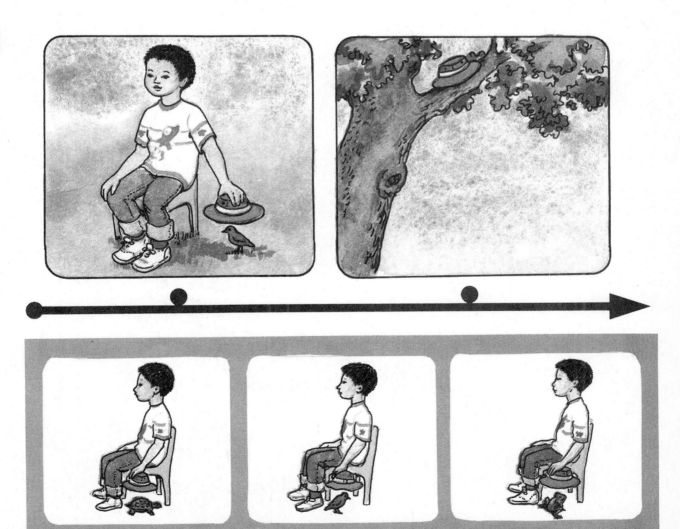

D

1.

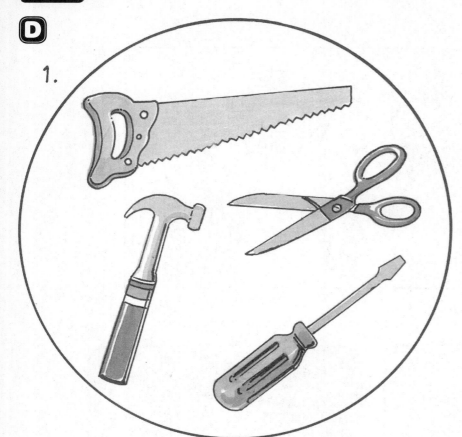

2.

E

1. true   false
2. true   false
3. true   false
4. true   false
5. true   false
6. true   false
7. true   false

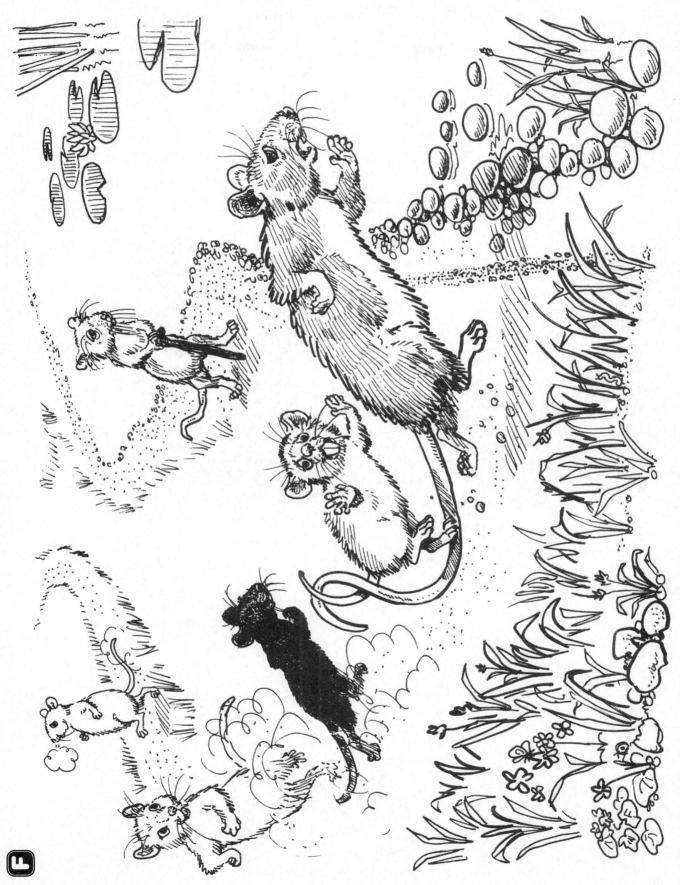

A

1. _____
2. _____
3. _____
4. _____
5. _____

B

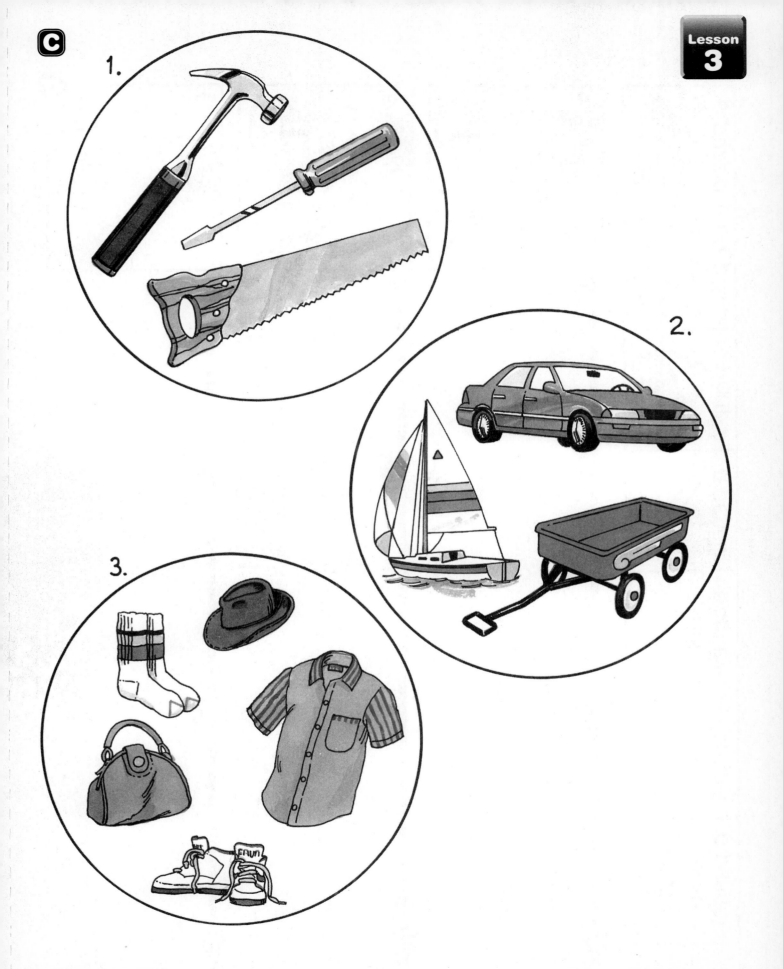

C

1.

2.

3.

D

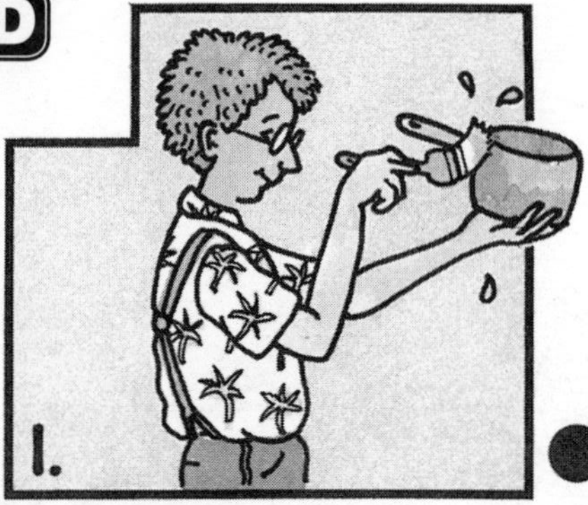
1.

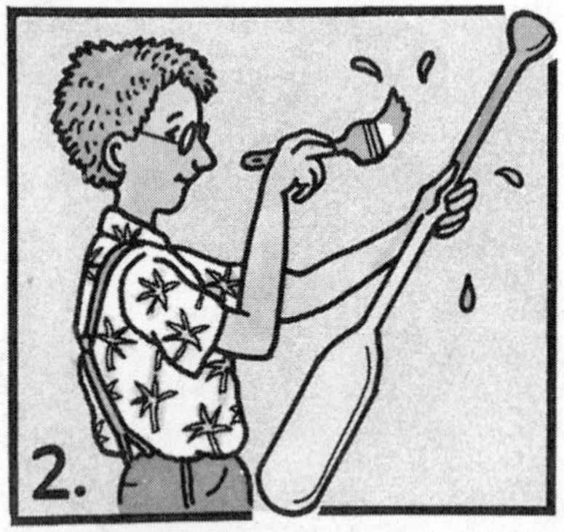
2.

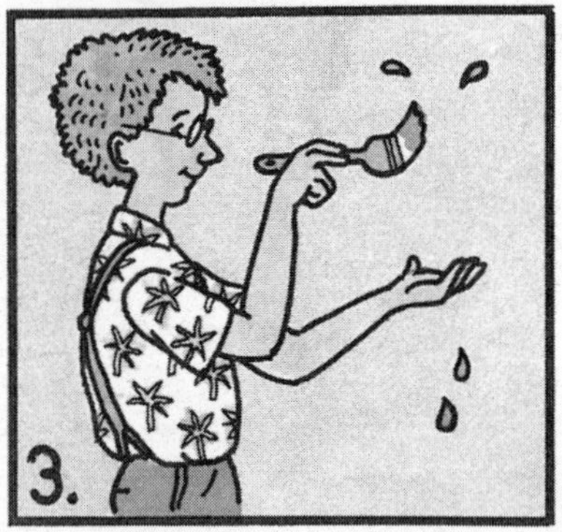
3.

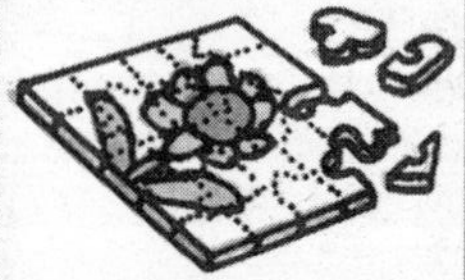 a puzzle	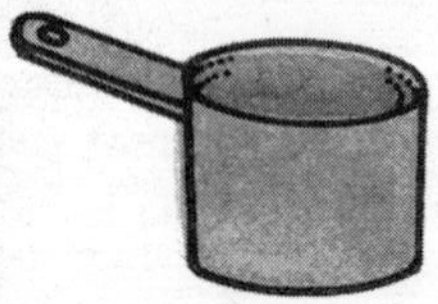 a pot	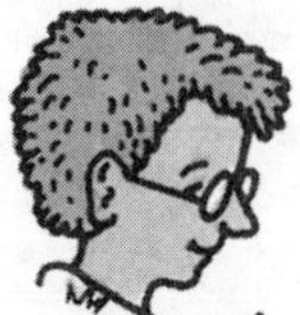 Paul	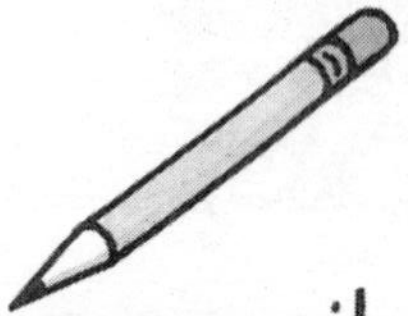 a pencil	painted	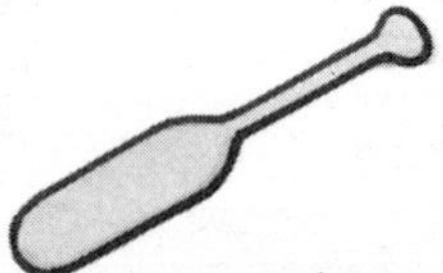 a paddle	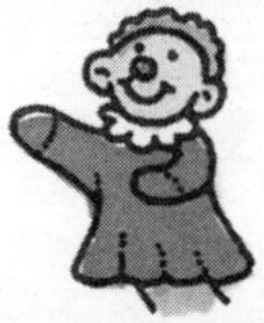 a puppet

E

A

	A boy was riding a bike.
	A girl ▓▓▓▓▓▓▓▓▓▓▓▓▓▓▓▓.

B

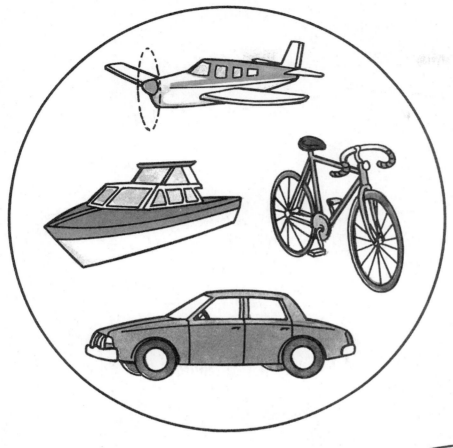

D

Ⓐ

	The girl rode an elephant.
	The boy ████████████████ .

B

Some of the bugs have spots.

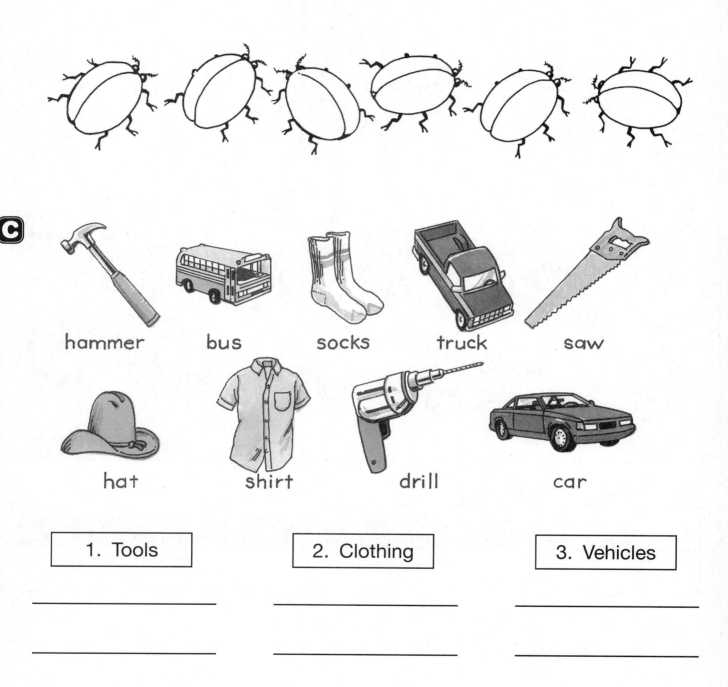

C

| hammer | bus | socks | truck | saw |

| hat | shirt | drill | car |

| 1. Tools | 2. Clothing | 3. Vehicles |

_____   _____   _____

_____   _____   _____

_____   _____   _____

Ⓐ

The boy read a paper.

██ .

B

1.

2.

A

carrot   owl   church   banana   turtle

bear   house   hamburger   barn

1. Food	2. Buildings	3. Animals
_____	_____	_____
_____	_____	_____
_____	_____	_____

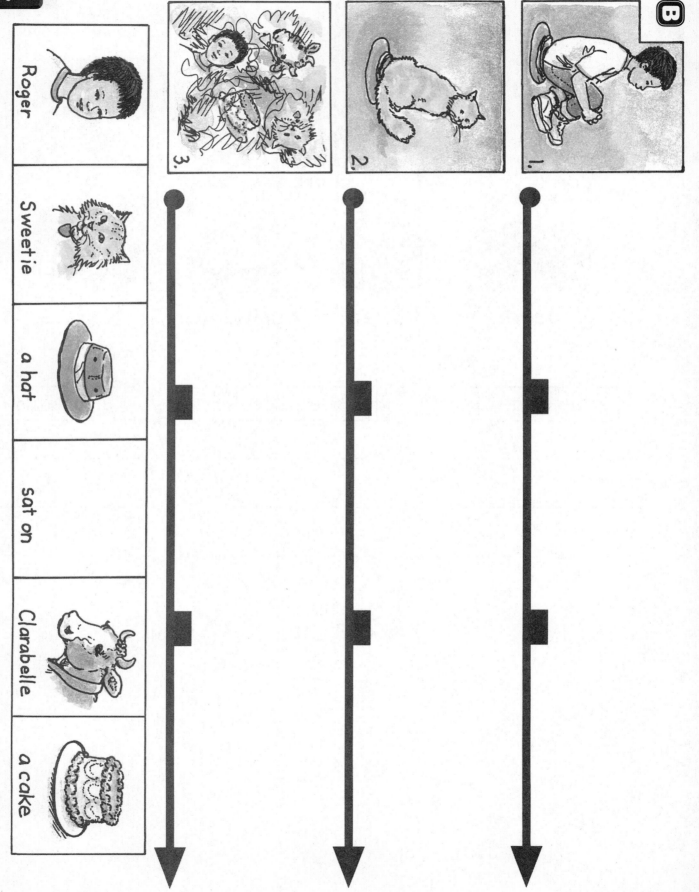

C

1. bud   2. yus   3. fud   4. ugg

Ⓐ

	The girl was standing on a chair.
	██████████████████████████████████████.

B

1. ●————————●————————▶

2.   ●————————●————————▶

C

1. egg shells

2. Ben met 5 men.

3. I had ten pets.

1.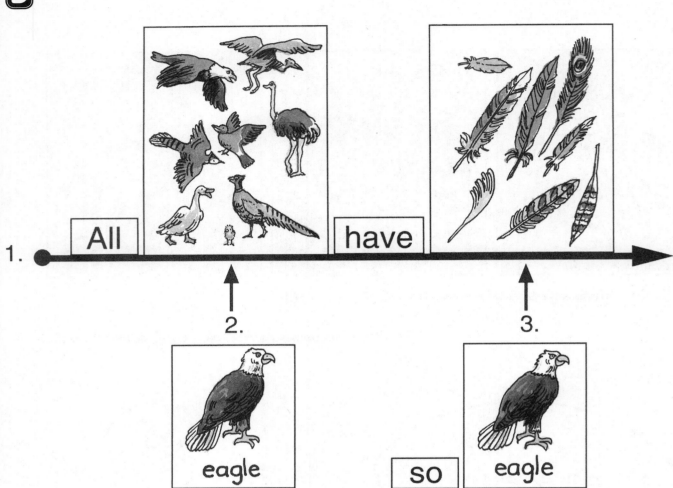

All   have

2.

eagle

3.

so   eagle

A

A cat was sleeping on the chair.

███.

B

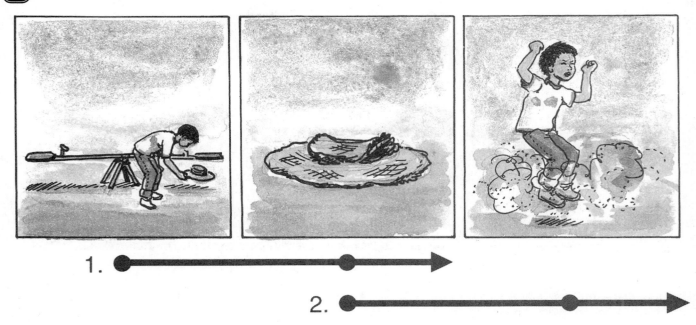

1. ●————————●————————▶

2.   ●————————————————●————————▶

C

a fan   a hat   a ball   a goat   a sheep   Clarabelle

1. The third object to Bleep's right is _____.

2. The first object to Bleep's left is _____.

3. The first object to Bleep's right is _____.

4. The second object to Bleep's _____ is a _____.

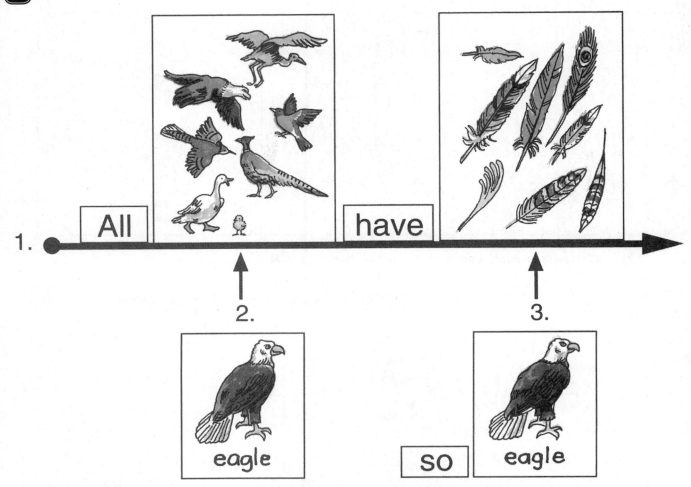

1. All have

2.

eagle

3.

SO eagle

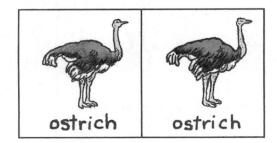

ostrich ostrich

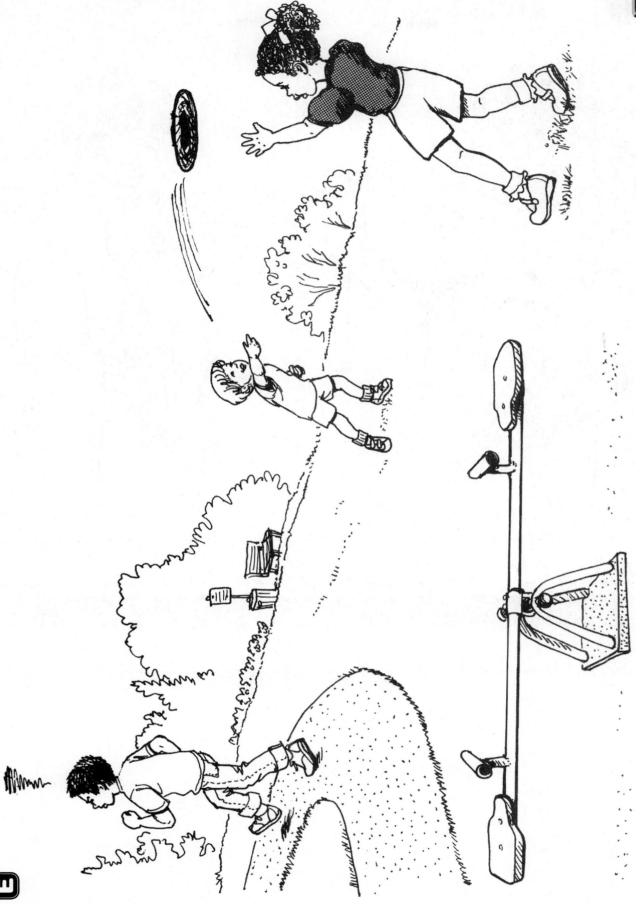

A

	The girl was drawing a picture.
	███████████████████████████████████ .

Test 1

B

a man   a sheep   a fan   a ball   a pig   a clock

1. The third object to Clarabelle's right is _____.

2. The third object to Clarabelle's left is _____.

3. The second object to Clarabelle's left is _____.

4. The first object to Clarabelle's right is _____.

C

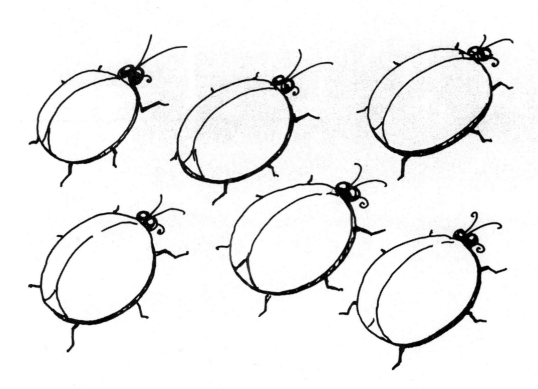

Lesson 10—Test 1   **33**

A

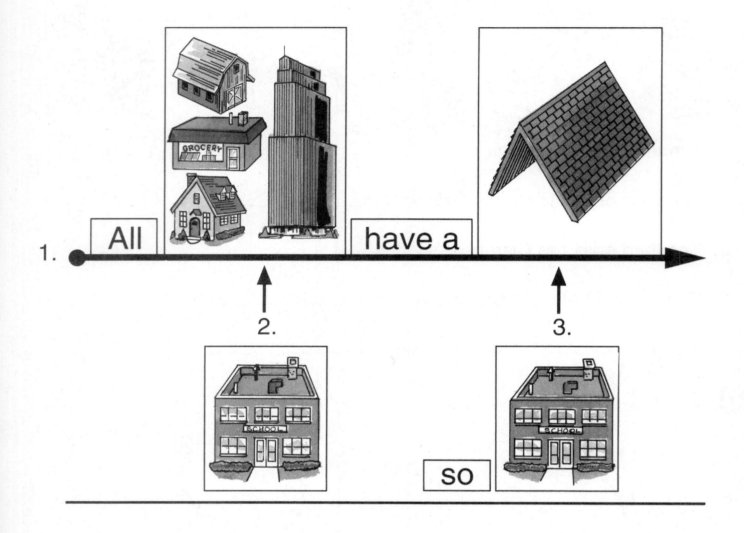

1.   All   have a

2.

3.

SCHOOL   so   SCHOOL

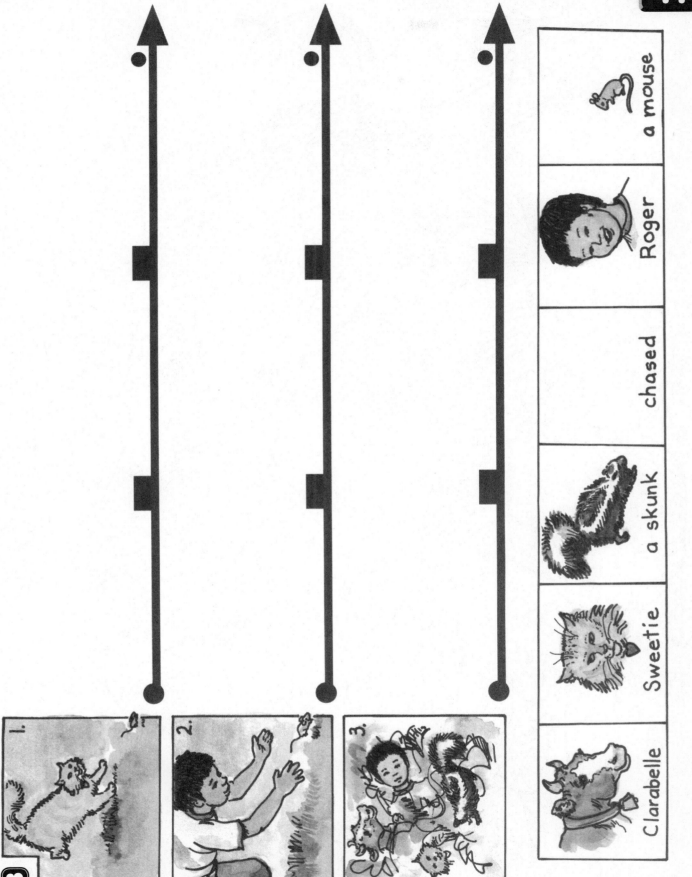

Ⓐ

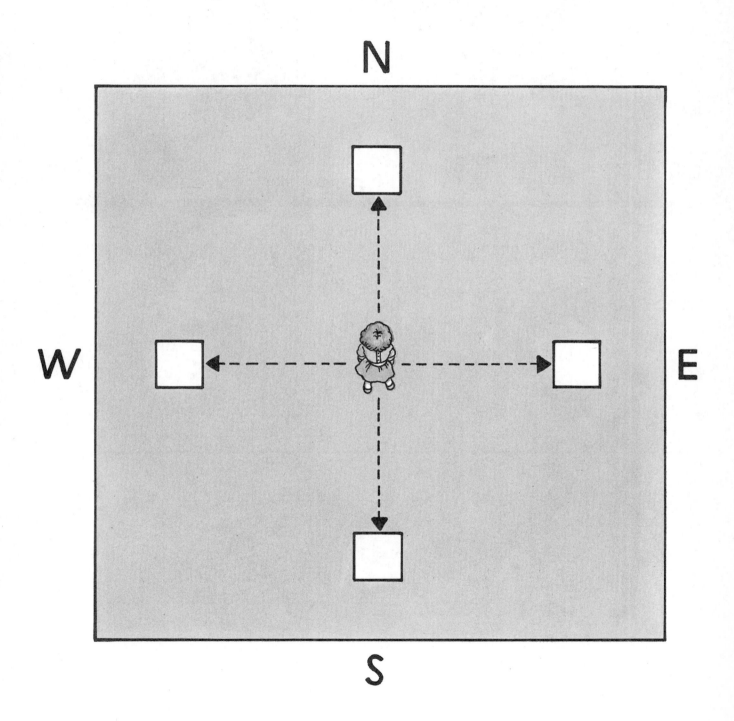

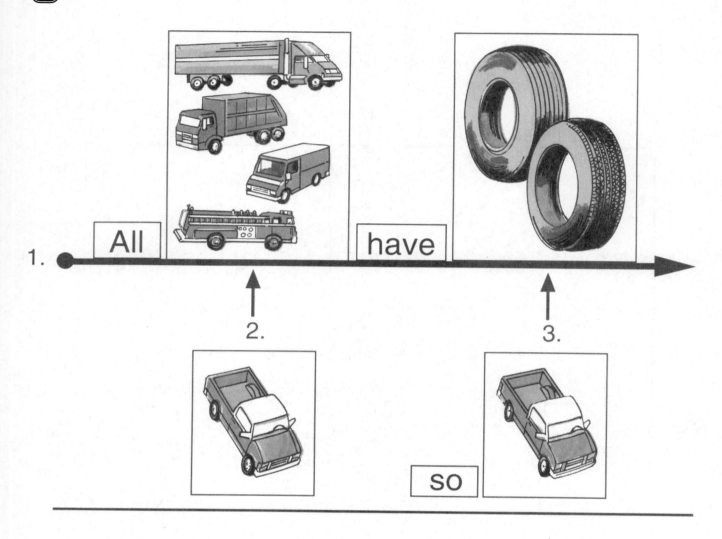

1. All ... have ...

2. ...

so 3. ...

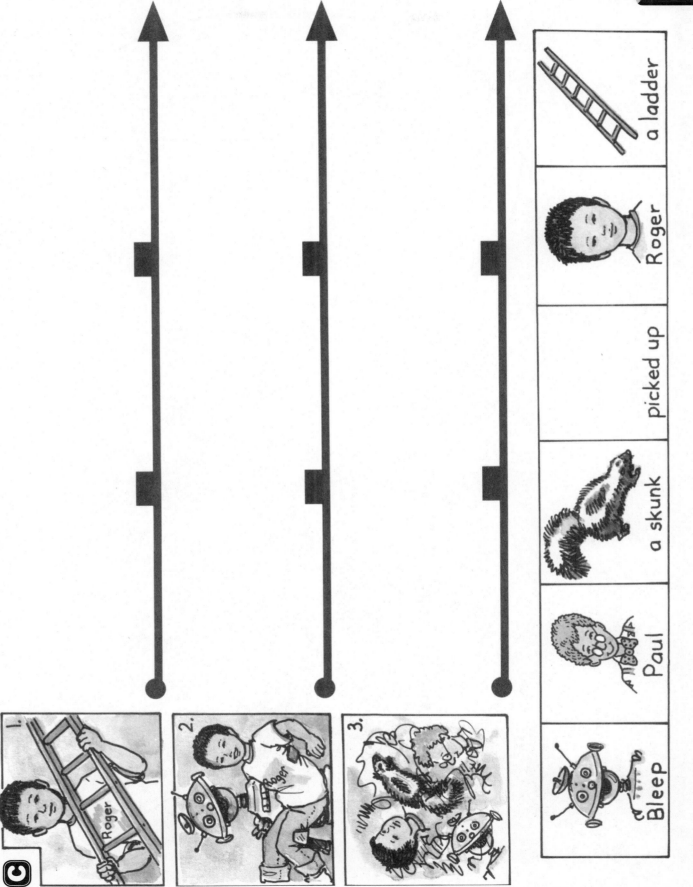

D

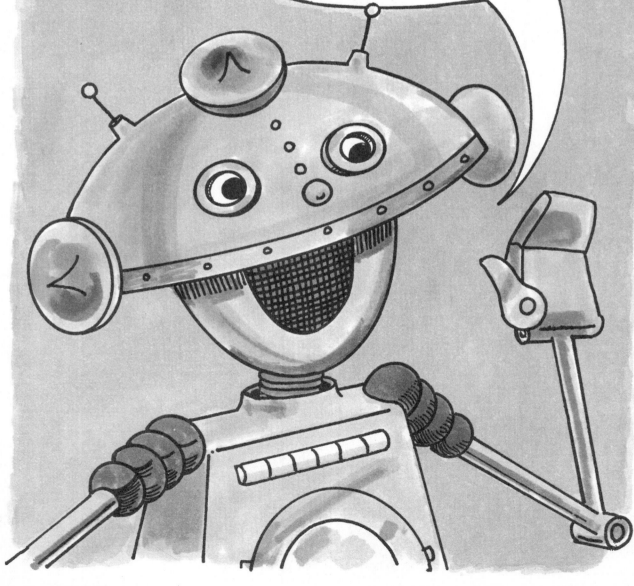

1. slide _____
2. slam _____
3. slug _____
4. sleep _____

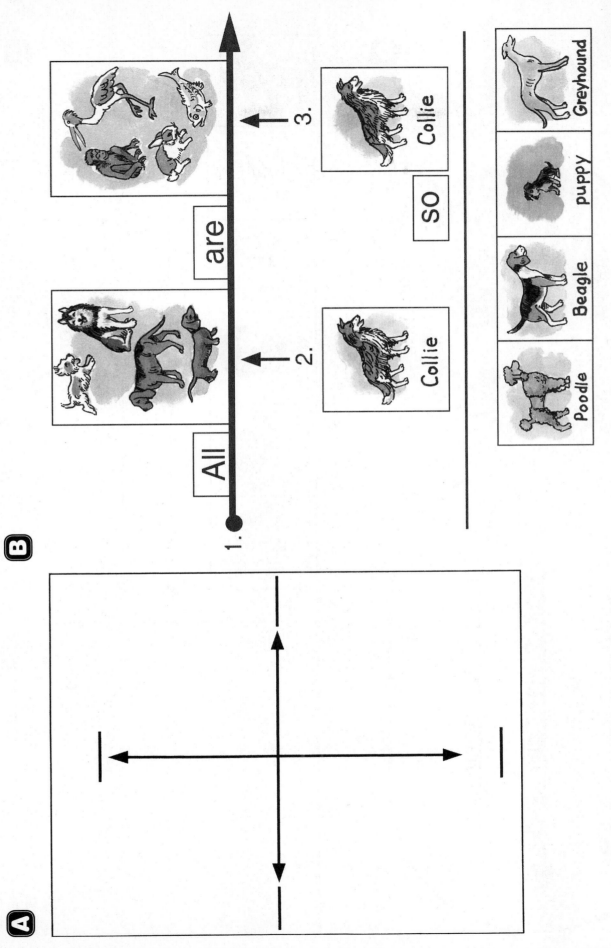

C

1. _____ sat on _____

2. _____ chased _____

3. _____ picked up _____

a skunk	Bleep	Sweetie	Roger	a hat	a toad

D

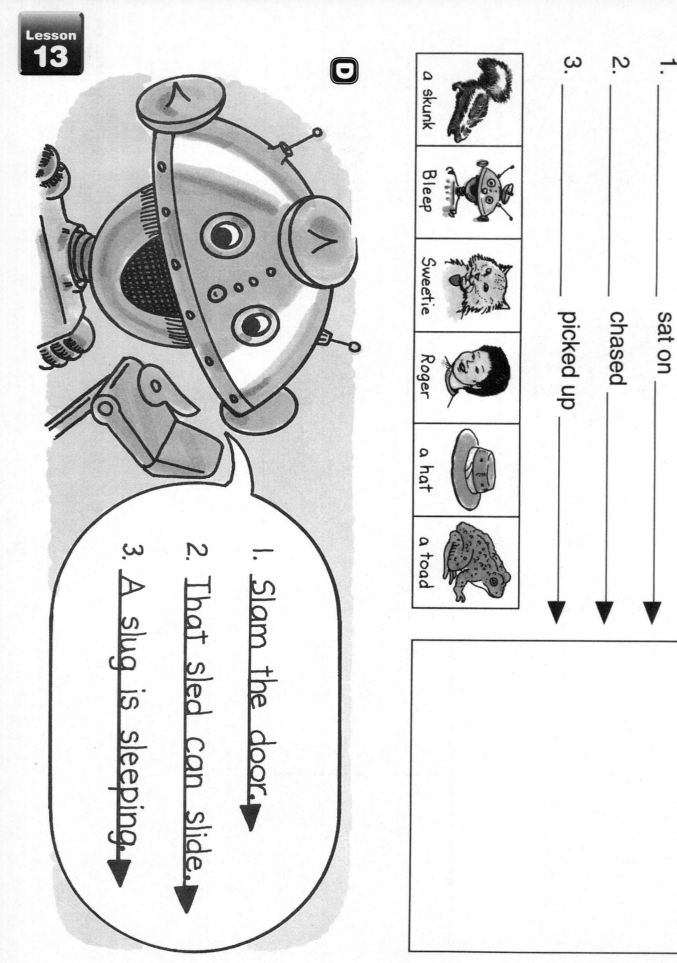

1. Slam the door.
2. That sled can slide.
3. A slug is sleeping.

A

milk	poured	some	banana	peeled

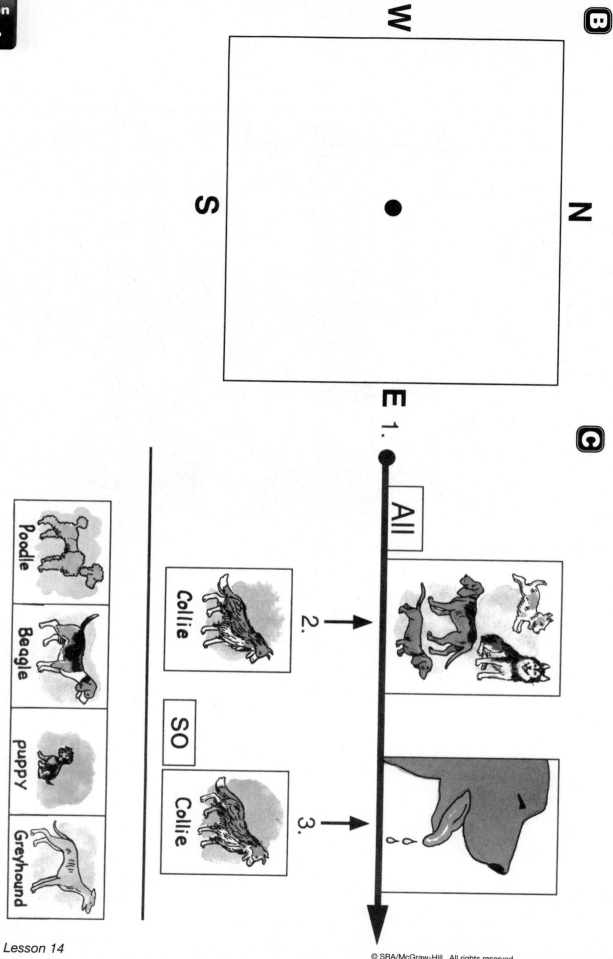

B

C

W

S   N

E   1.

All

2. →

Collie

SO

3. →

Collie

Poodle   Beagle   puppy   Greyhound

A

N

W

E

S

B

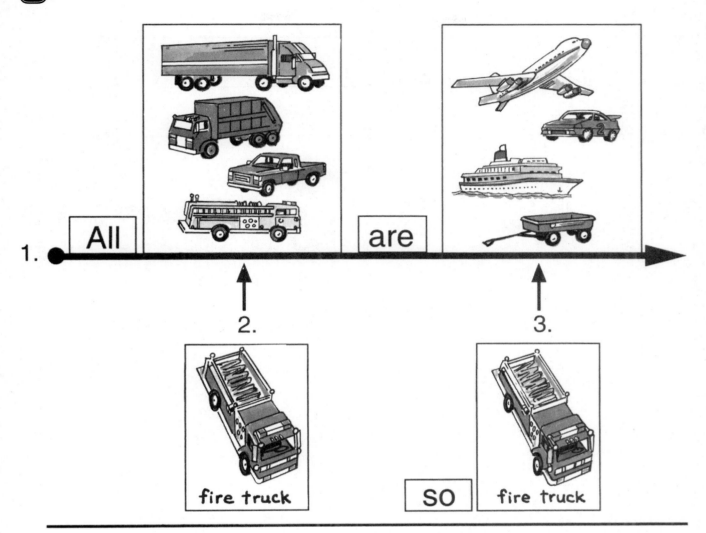

1. All _____ are _____

2. fire truck

SO 3. fire truck

C

1. _____ hugged _____ ➤

2. _____ washed _____ ➤

3. _____ talked to _____ ➤

a skunk	Sweetie	a hat	Roger	a clown	Bleep

A

an apple	an orange	peeled	ate

B

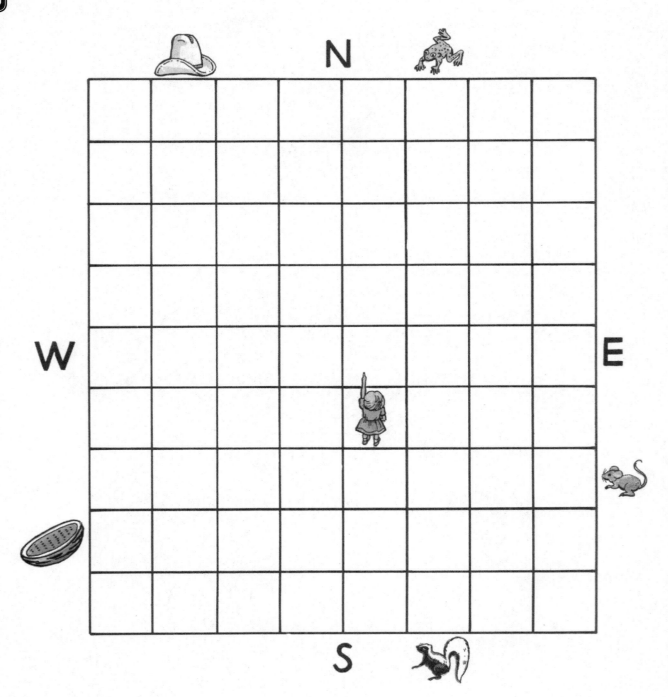

1. Owen   a little person
2. Owen   a little person
3. Owen   a little person
4. Owen   a little person

A

1. _____ smelled _____ ▶

2. _____ held _____ ▶

3. _____ kissed _____ ▶

| the soap | Goober | a skunk | Molly |
| Owen | a hat | Bleep | Clarabelle |

B

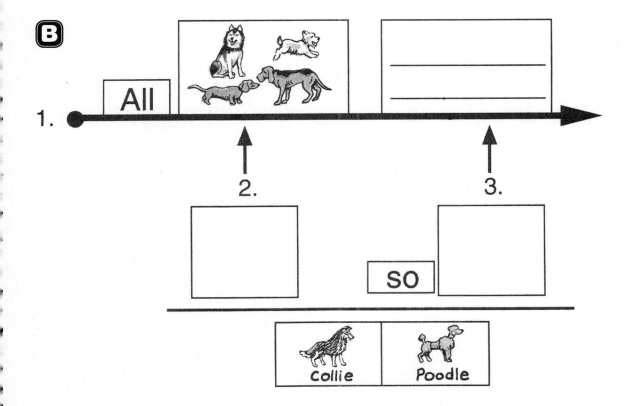

1.

All

2.

3.

SO

Collie   Poodle

C

Dear

D

Dear Owen,
Our names are Fizz and Liz
~~Hello, my name is Owen~~

we
and ~~I~~ live on a beautiful island.

This island is very small.

There are many small animals

on this island.

We have tiny bears and tigers

and alligators.

We have tiny rabbits.

We also have lots of tiny birds.

The biggest of the tiny birds

is the eagle.

We have bugs that are so small

you can hardly see them.

Ⓐ

| standing | sitting | table | wagon |

B

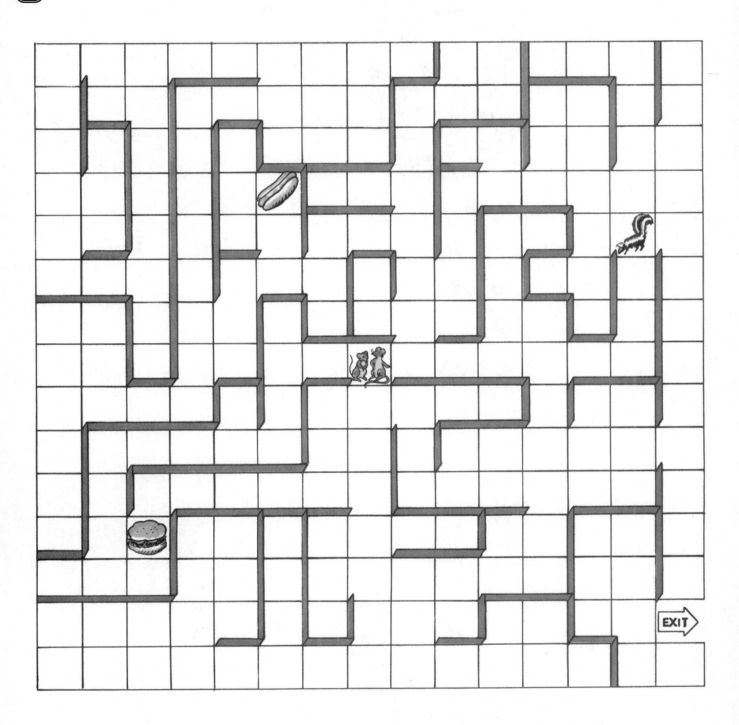

A

climbed	chewed	bone

Bragging Rat

Bragging Rat

1. Two squares to the north.

2. Three squares to the east.

3. Three squares to the south.

4. Four squares to the west.

1. Two squares to the north.

2. Three squares to the west.

3. Three squares to the south.

4. Four squares to the west.

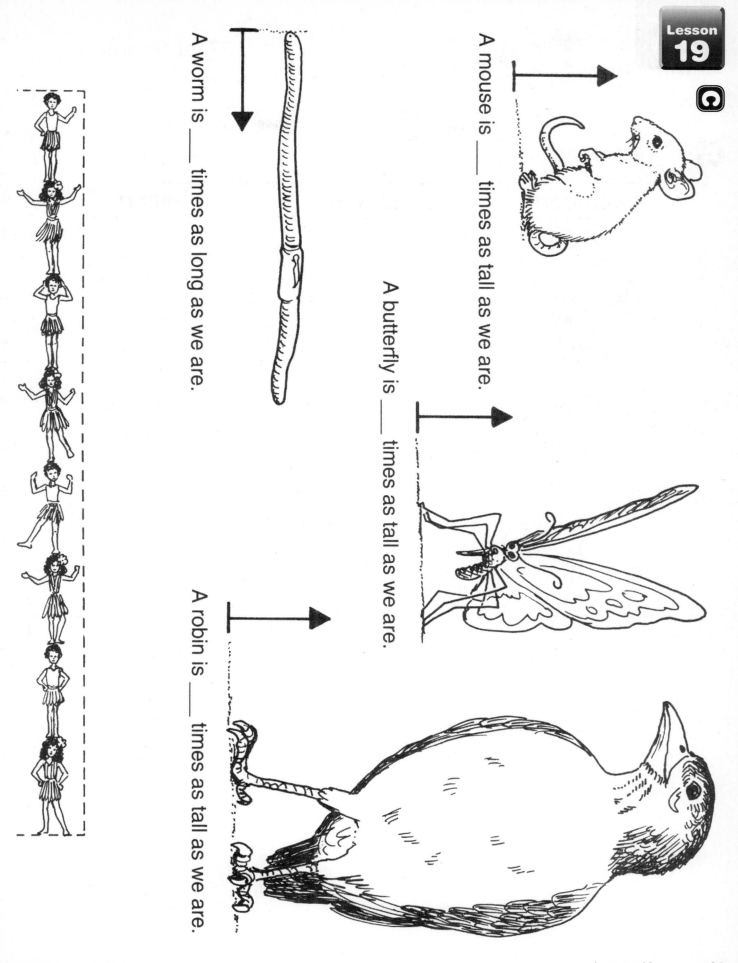

A mouse is ____ times as tall as we are.

A butterfly is ____ times as tall as we are.

A worm is ____ times as long as we are.

A robin is ____ times as tall as we are.

A

| popcorn | reading | eating |

Test 2

B

north

east

south

west

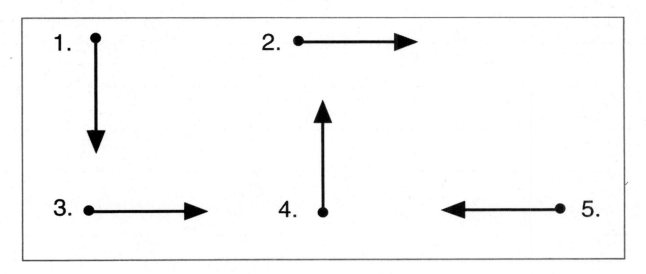

1. Arrow 1 points _____.

2. Arrow 2 points _____.

3. Arrow 3 points _____.

4. Arrow 4 points _____.

5. Arrow 5 points _____.

A

1.

_____

_____

_____

2.

_____

_____

_____

3.

_____

_____

_____

_____

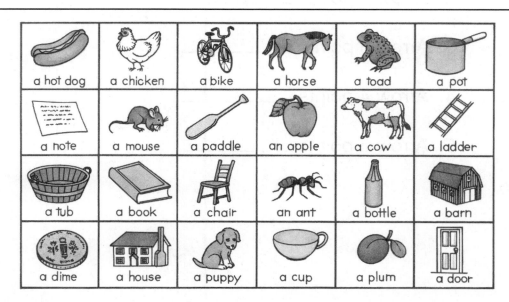

a hot dog	a chicken	a bike	a horse	a toad	a pot
a note	a mouse	a paddle	an apple	a cow	a ladder
a tub	a book	a chair	an ant	a bottle	a barn
a dime	a house	a puppy	a cup	a plum	a door

B

Ⓐ

| next | box | chair |

B

Hounds

1. Greyhound
2. Beagle
3. Basset

Work Dogs

1. Collie
2. German shepherd
3. Saint Bernard

C

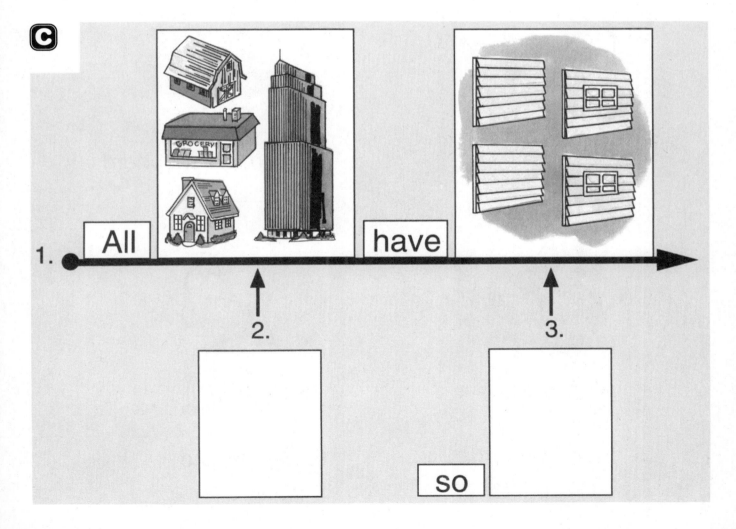

1. All ... have ...

2.

3.

SO

A

1. Basset

_____

2. Collie

_____

3. Beagle

_____

4. German shepherd

_____

5. Saint Bernard

_____

6. Greyhound

_____

B

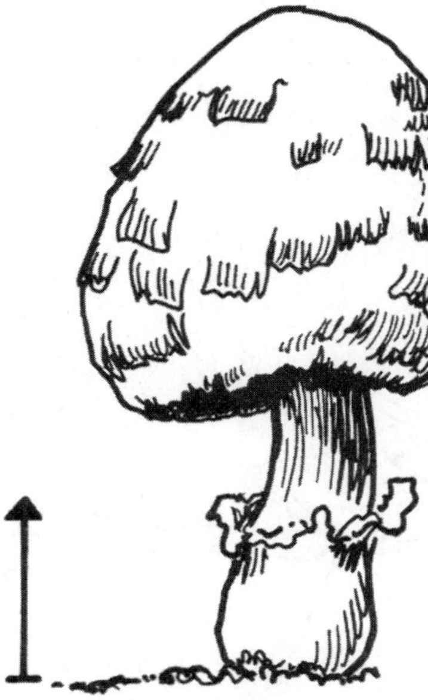

toadstool

banana

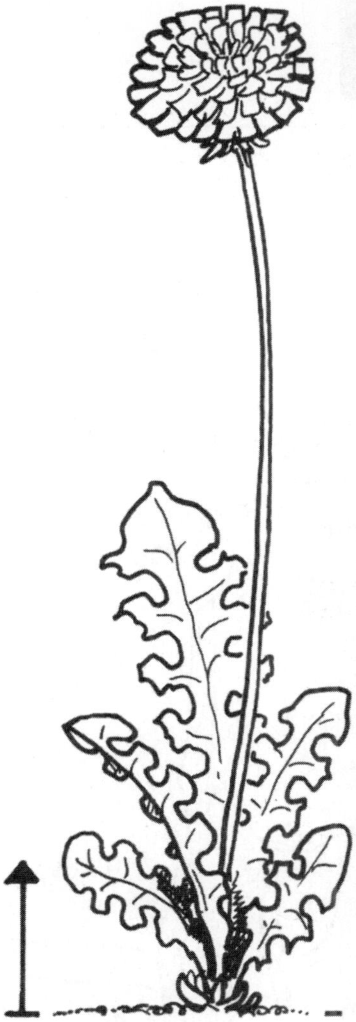

dandelion

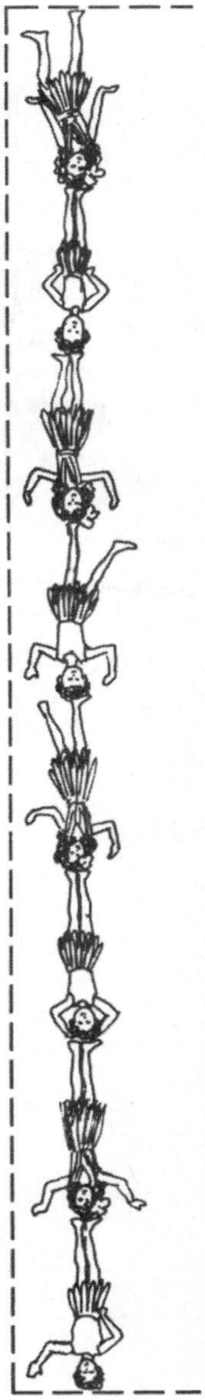

———————————,

_____

_____

_____

_____

_____

_____

A | sawed   painted   woman   board

Not-Class

Class

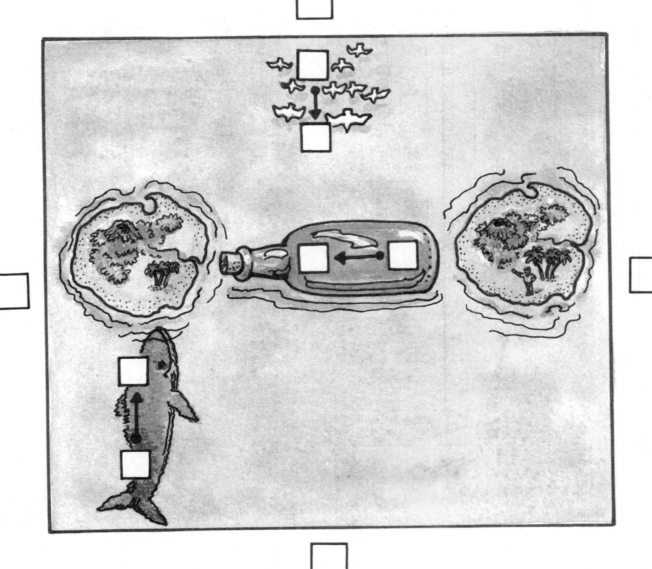

toadstools

 Where is Jenny the toad in the afternoon?

- In the afteroon, all the toads are _____

- Jenny is _____

- So in the afternoon, Jenny is _____

berry bush

 Where is Rod the red bug in the afternoon?

- In the afternoon, all the red bugs are _____

- Rod is _____

- So in the afternoon, Rod is _____

1.

_____

_____

_____

2.

_____

_____

_____

3.

_____

_____

_____

Lesson 26

B

a truck	a horse	Clarabelle	a skunk	in
Roger	water	a tent	a tree	under
a barn	Owen	a tub	a cage	between
an elephant	a pond	a hole	Molly	next to
a birdbath	a basket	a junkyard	a fishbowl	on
Fizz & Liz	a bottle	a mountain	a bike	over
a ski lodge	an island	a boat	a train	behind
a toadstool	a toaster	a violin	a cow	to
a store	a garage	an airplane	a lake	up
Paul	a box	a ladder	Goober	down

A

B

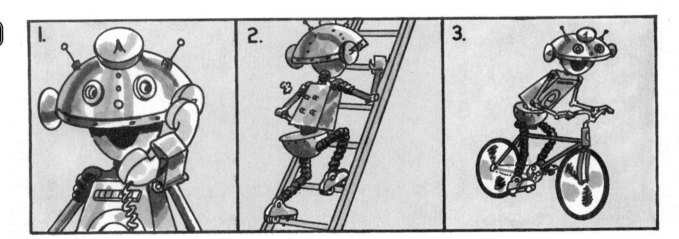

1. Bleep climbed a ladder after he _____

_____.

2. Bleep rode a bike after he _____

_____.

Ⓒ

Class

Not-Class

1. _____

2. _____

3. _____

1. Clarabelle jumped into a pond after she _____

   _____.

2. Clarabelle climbed a tree after she _____

   _____.

B

oak tree

lily pads

A. Where is Bonnie the bluebird in the afternoon?

   1. In the afternoon, all the bluebirds are in the oak tree.

   2. Bonnie is a _____.

   3. So in the afternoon, _____.

B. Where is Fran the frog in the afternoon?

   1. In the afternoon, all the frogs are _____.

   2. Fran is a _____.

   3. So in the afternoon, _____.

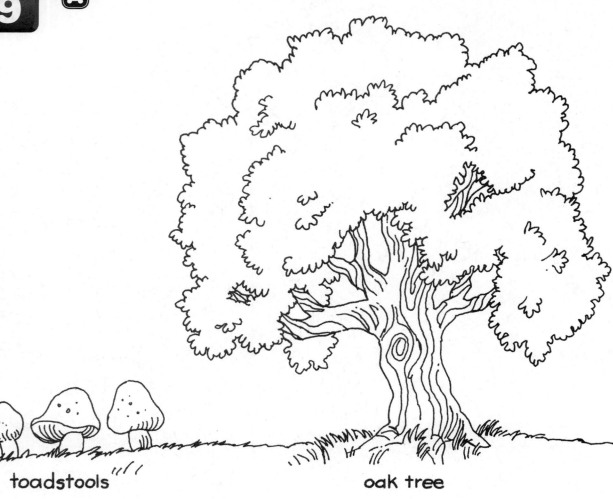

toadstools

oak tree

A. Where is Tammy the toad in the morning?

1. In the morning, all the toads are _____.

2. Tammy is a _____.

3. So in the morning, Tammy is _____.

B. Where is Bonnie the bluebird in the morning?

1. In the morning, all the bluebirds are _____.

2. Bonnie is a _____.

3. So in the morning, Bonnie is _____.

B

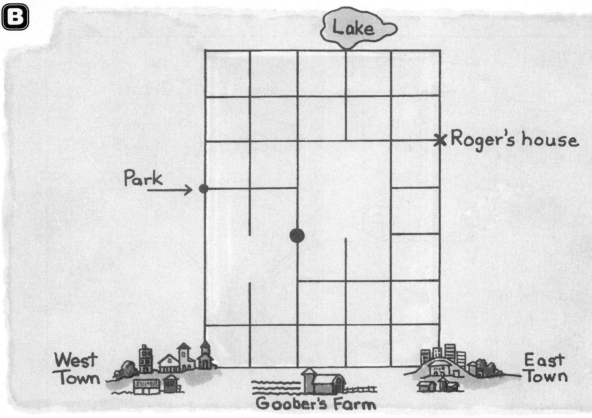

1. To go to Roger's house, you go _____ miles _____.

   Then you go _____ miles _____.

2. To go to West Town, you go _____ miles _____.

   Then you go _____ miles _____.

C

Collie   Saint Bernard

Test 3

Test Score [ ]

A | skipped   catch   played   rope

Test 3

Test 3

C

toadstools   oak tree   lily pads

A. Where is Fran the frog in the afternoon?

  1. In the afternoon, all the frogs are _____.

  2. Fran is a _____.

  3. So in the afternoon, Fran is _____.

B. Where is Bonnie the bluebird in the afternoon?

  1. In the afternoon, all the bluebirds are _____.

  2. Bonnie is a _____.

  3. So in the afternoon, Bonnie is _____.

C. Where is Tammy the toad in the afternoon?

  1. In the afternoon, all the toads are _____.

  2. Tammy is a _____.

  3. So in the afternoon, Tammy is _____.

Lesson 31

ball   end

go   ant

dig   candy

fill

1. _____

2. _____

3. _____

4. _____

5. _____

6. _____

7. _____

     Lesson 32   **89**

B

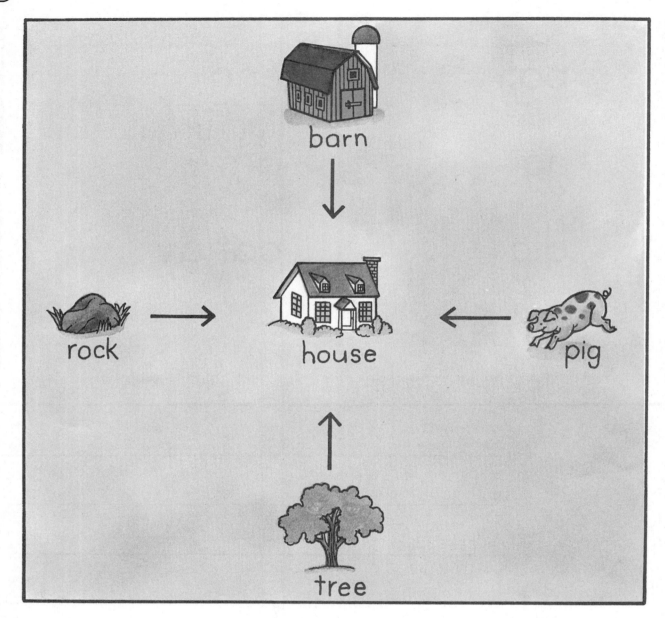

1. The house is west of _____.

2. The house is north of _____.

3. The house is east of _____.

4. The house is south of _____.

Class

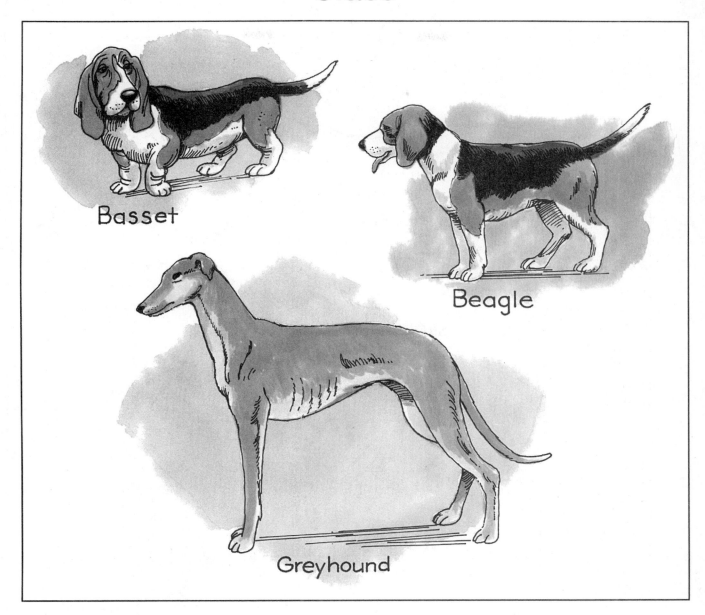

_____ hounds

_____ fast-running hounds

_____ dogs

_____ animals

A

line

ground

it

moon

help

kitchen

jumps

1. _____

2. _____

3. _____

4. _____

5. _____

6. _____

7. _____

B

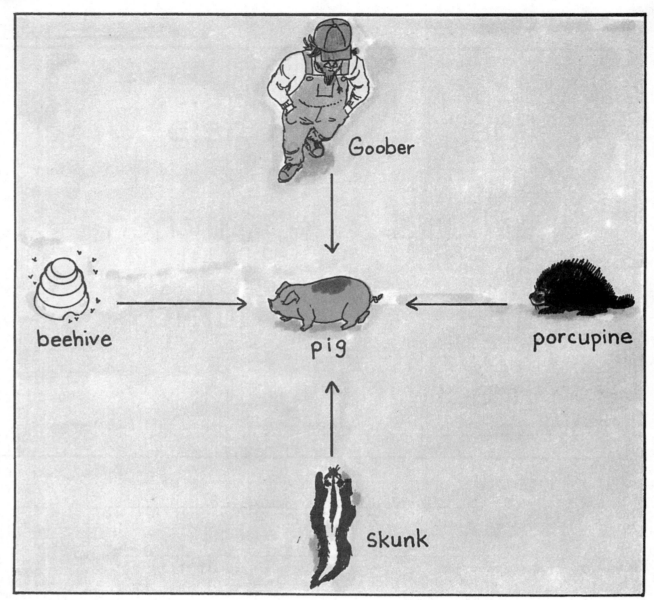

1. The pig is south of _____.

2. The pig is north of _____.

3. The pig is west of _____.

4. The pig is east of _____.

Class

Collie

Saint Bernard

German shepherd

_____ work dogs

_____ animals

_____ work dogs with ears that stand straight up

_____ dogs

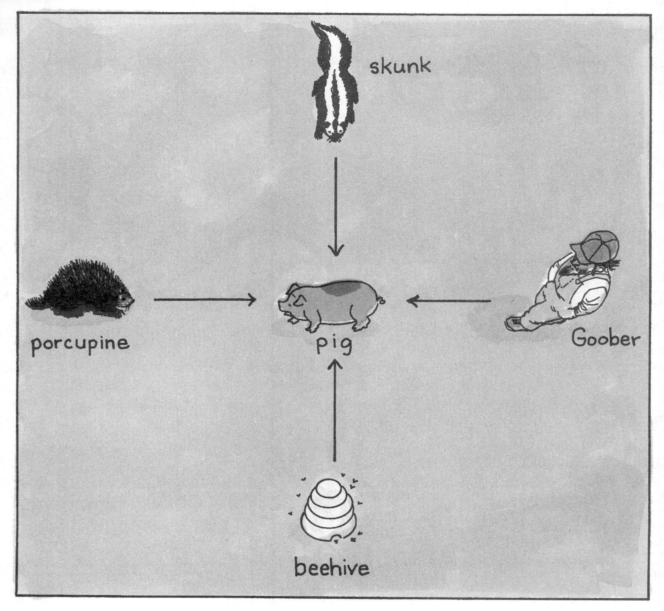

1. The pig is east of _____.

2. The pig is north of _____.

3. The pig is west of _____.

4. The pig is south of _____.

B

1. Goober _____
   after he milked a cow.

2. Goober _____
   after he played the violin.

3. Goober _____
   after he took a bath.

C

1. My brother and my sister had pet pigs. <u>They</u> just loved to roll around in the mud.

2. We always kept a glass on top of the refrigerator. We kept <u>it</u> full of water.

A

helpful

knock

jumpy

gate

farmer

landed

inside

1. _____

2. _____

3. _____

4. _____

5. _____

6. _____

7. _____

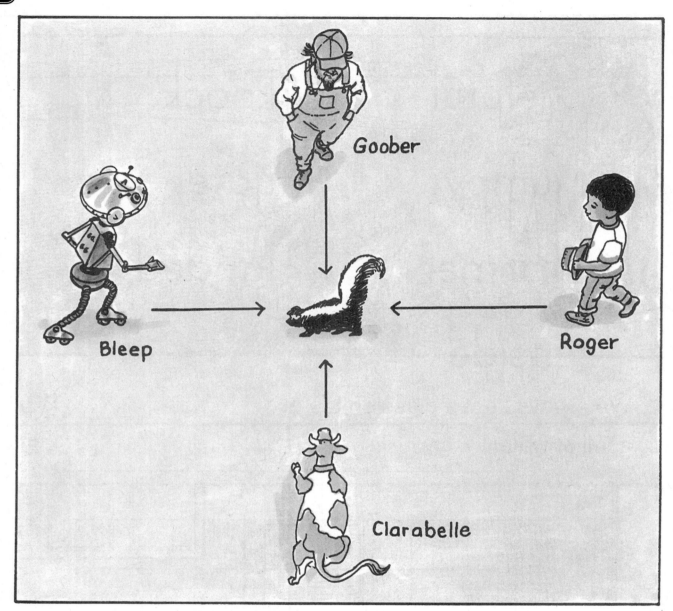

1. The skunk is north of _____.

2. The skunk is east of _____.

3. The skunk is west of _____.

4. The skunk is south of _____.

C

A.

This thing is in the class of bikes.

_____

B.

This thing is in the class of black bikes.

_____

C.

This thing is in the class of black bikes with a flat front tire.

_____

D.

This thing is in the class of black bikes with a flat front tire and

_____

_____.

1.

2.

3.

4.

5.

6.

7.

8.

D

1. My brother and my sister had pet pigs. <u>They</u> just loved to roll around in the mud.

2. We always kept a glass on top of the refrigerator. We kept <u>it</u> full of water.

A

jaws   oldest

lake   kitten

nothing   meaning

ice

1. _____

2. _____

3. _____

4. _____

5. _____

6. _____

7. _____

C

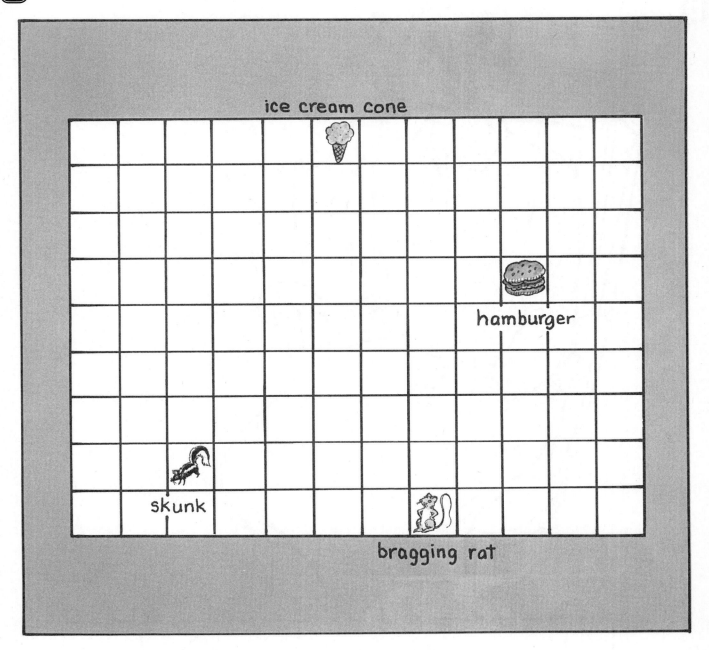

Step A.　　4 squares north

Step B.　　3 squares west

Step C.　　4 squares north

Step D.　　2 squares west

Step E.　　7 squares south

The bragging rat ended up at the _____.

Mother held Baby Sarah as <u>she</u> drank from a baby bottle.

D

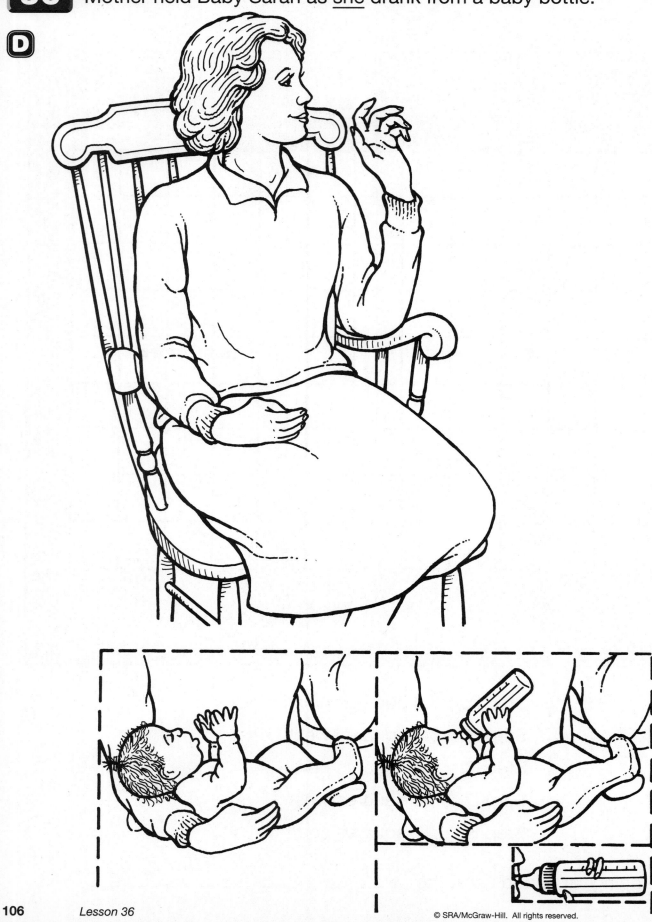

A

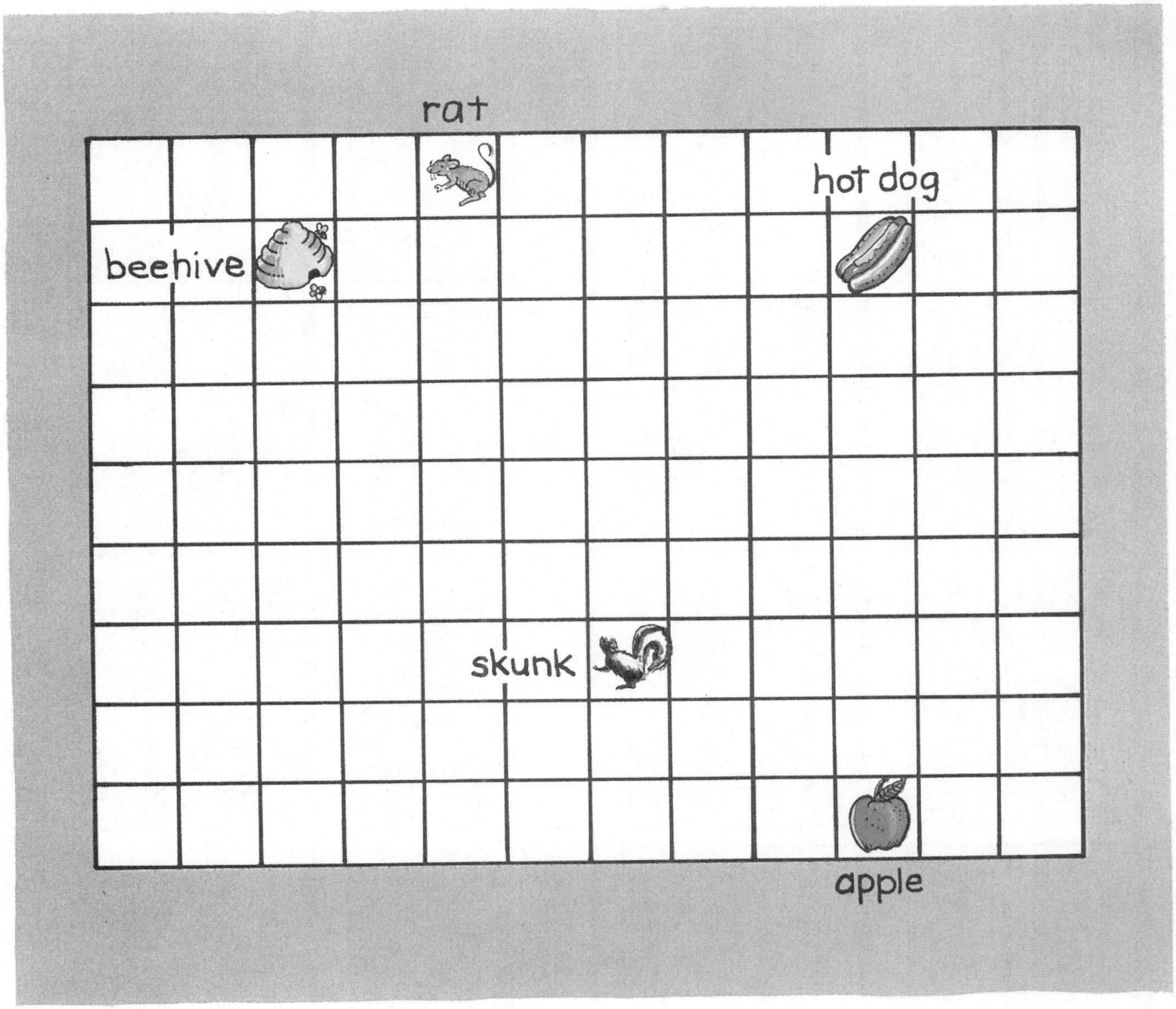

rat

hot dog

beehive

skunk

apple

Step A.　　3 squares north

Step B.　　1 square east

Step C.　　1 square south

Step D.　　3 squares west

Step E.　　4 squares north

The skunk ended up at the _____.

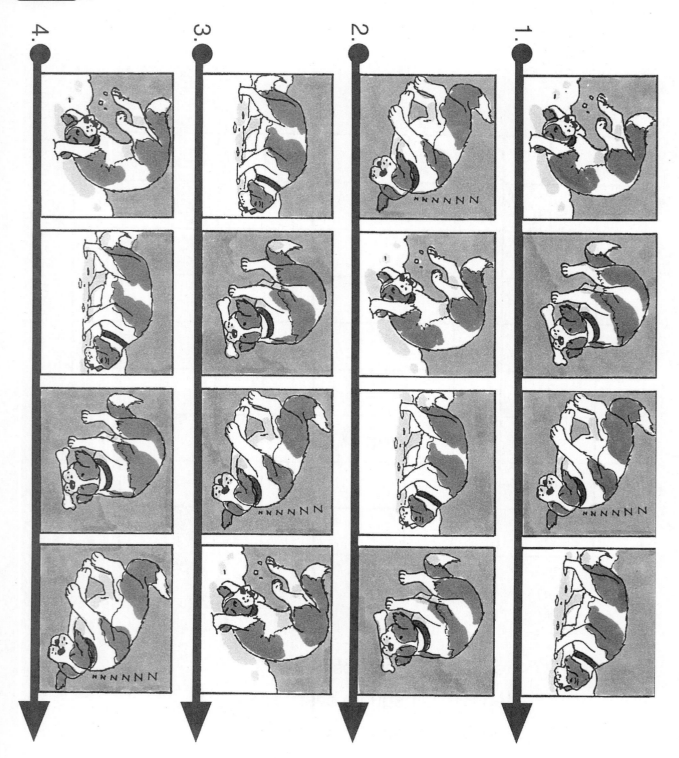

C

Lesson **37**

1. Our car made a dust cloud. It floated away.

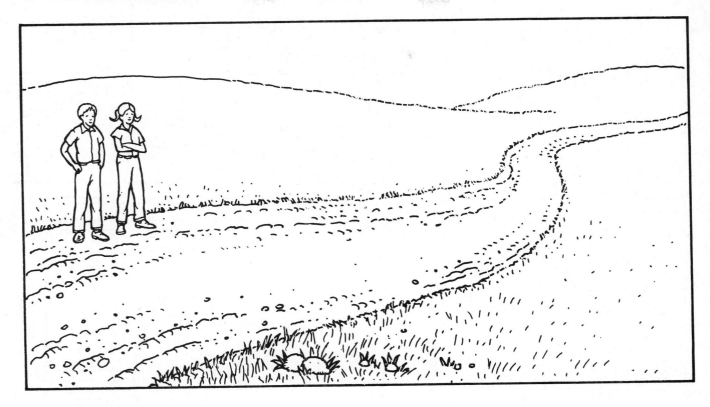

2. A frog was on top of the car. It had big black spots all over.

Lesson 37 **109**

D

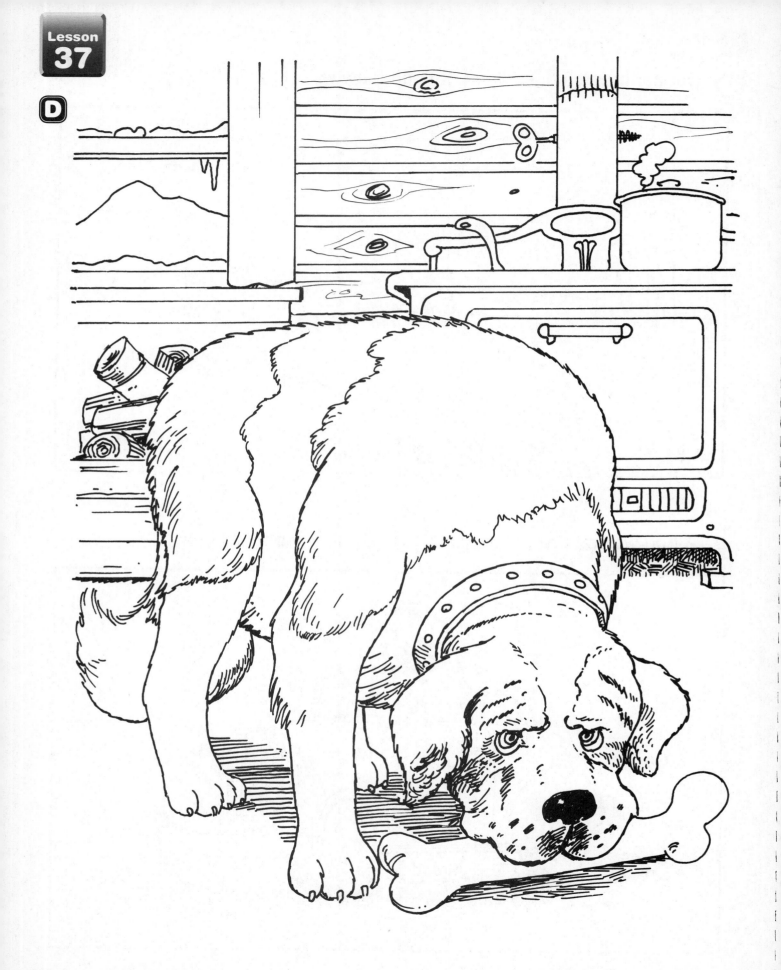

A

restful question

pound until

older thing

something

1. _____

2. _____

3. _____

4. _____

5. _____

6. _____

7. _____

B

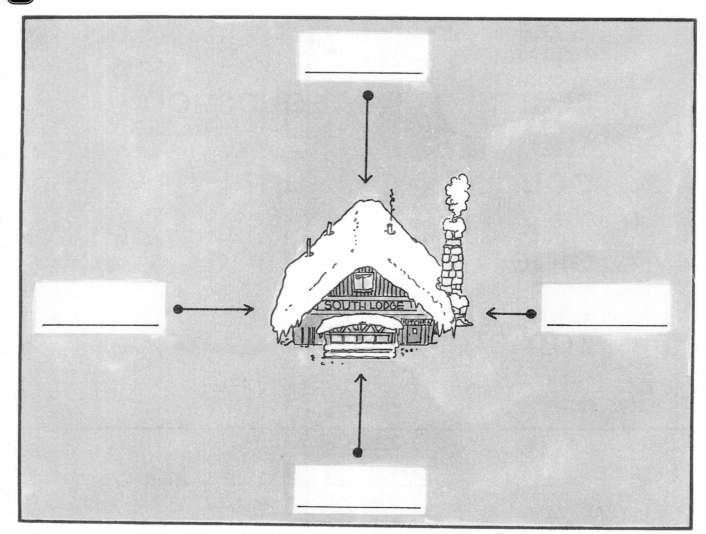

Zelda

Bleep

Dot

Molly

C

We had a fence next to the barn. Our dog jumped over it.

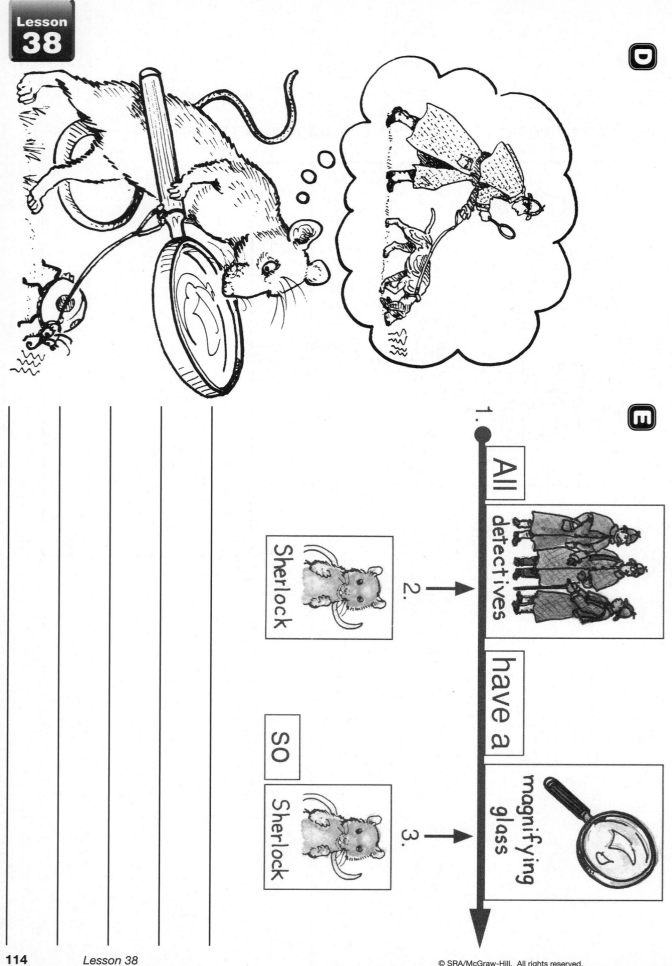

1. All detectives have a magnifying glass

2. Sherlock

3. so Sherlock

A

wishful   ugly

time   x-ray

zoo   van

yawning

1. _____

2. _____

3. _____

4. _____

5. _____

6. _____

7. _____

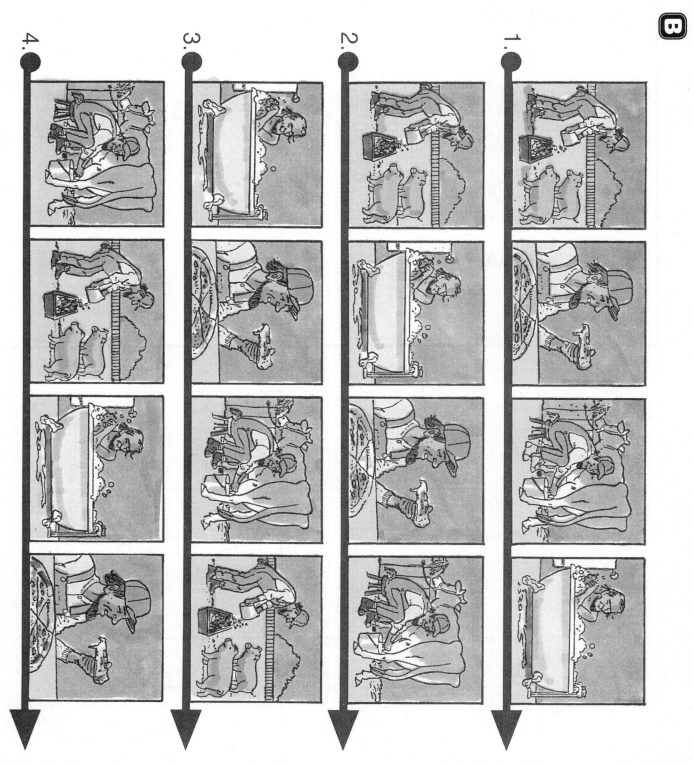

C

My brothers had dogs. They loved to carry a bone around in their mouth.

D

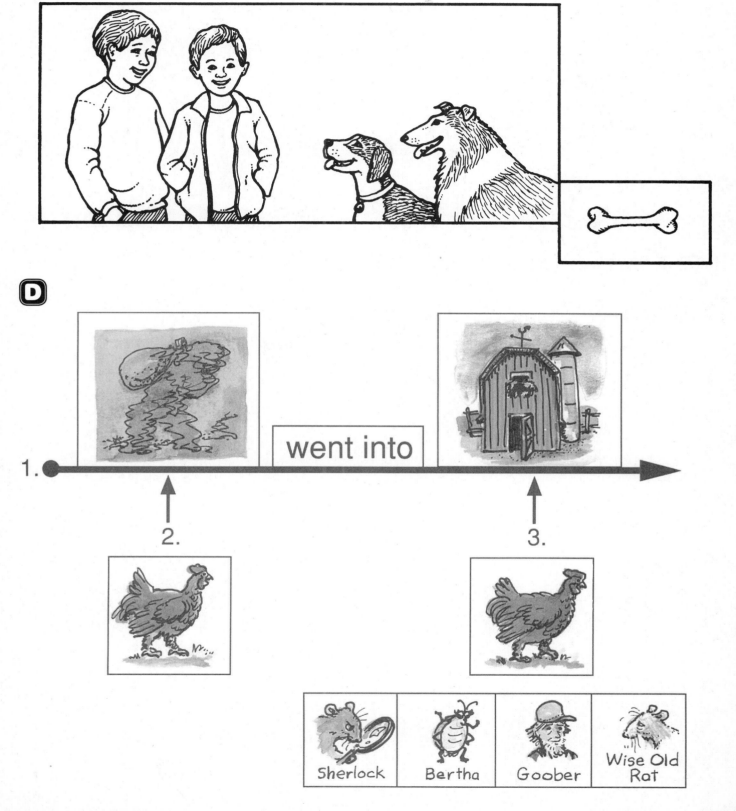

went into

1.

2.

3.

Sherlock   Bertha   Goober   Wise Old Rat

A | chair | woman | sitting | painting |

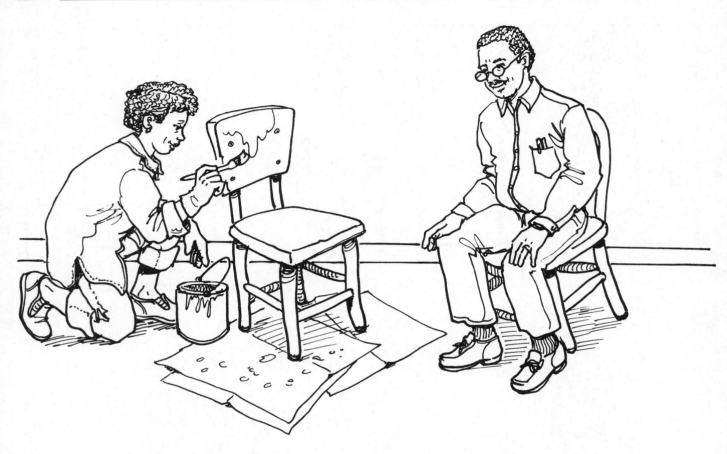

Test 4

B

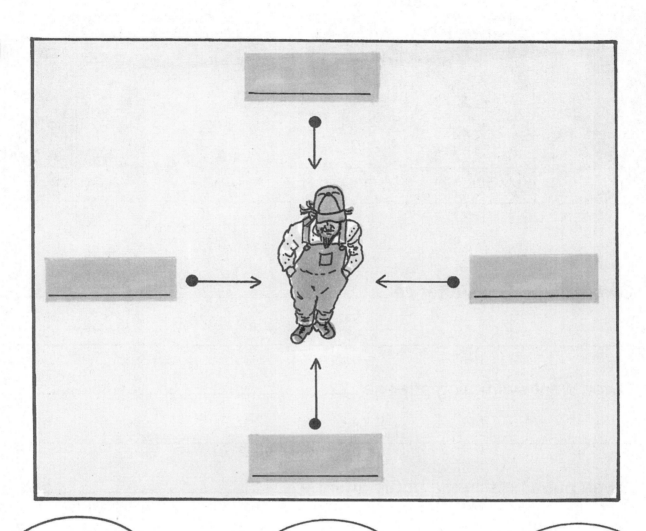

Goober is north.

Dud

Goober is west.

Ranger

Goober is south.

Bleep

Test 4

C

1. Owen ate bananas after he _____

   _____.

2. Owen went swimming after he _____

   _____.

3. Owen put a note in the bottle after he _____

   _____.

D

1. boys   children
2. animals   cows
3. fruit   apples

A

rode	horse	bike	girl

B

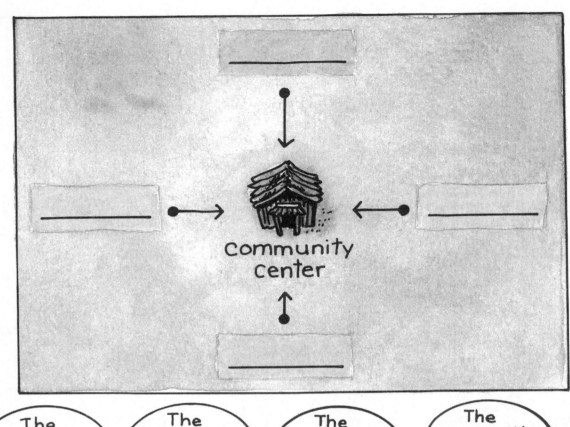

The community center is east.

Sherlock

The community center is south.

Bertha

The community center is west.

Zelda

The community center is north.

Owen

Lesson
41

1. Aunt Mary put her pie near the stool and Wilber sat on it.

2. Uncle Henry talked to little Billy as he shaved.

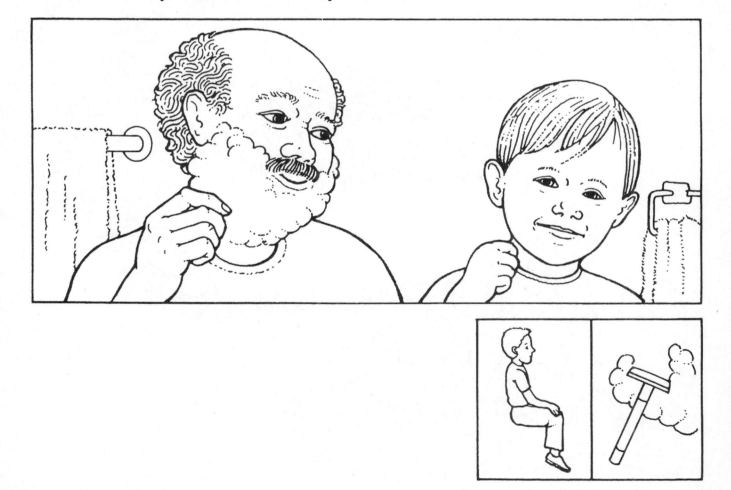

Lesson 41 **123**

Lesson 41

Ⓐ

mopped	washed	dishes	floor

When the boys petted the dogs, they wagged their tails.

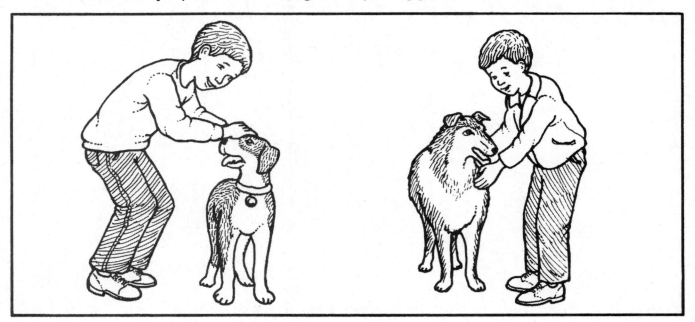

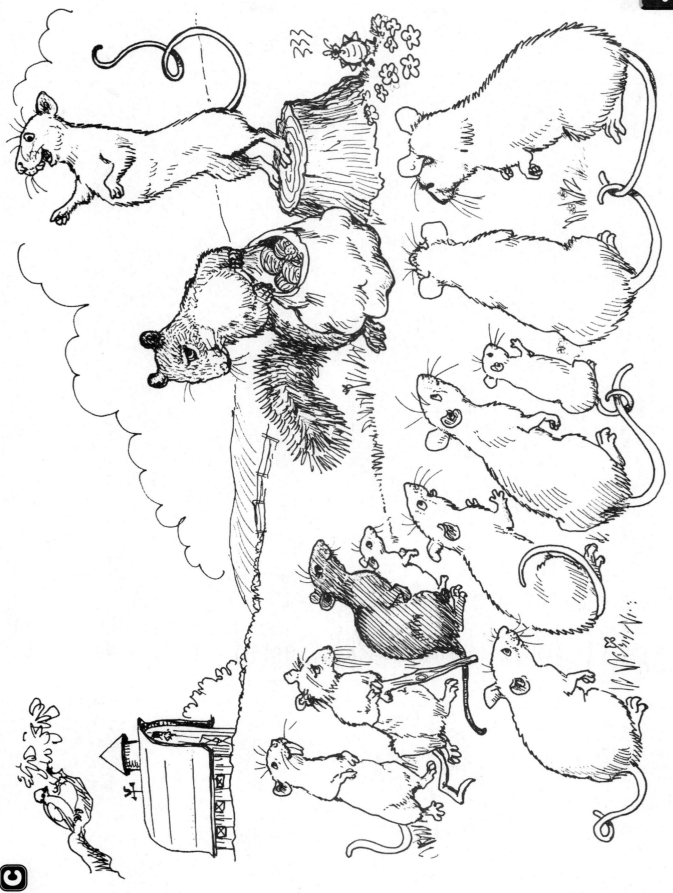

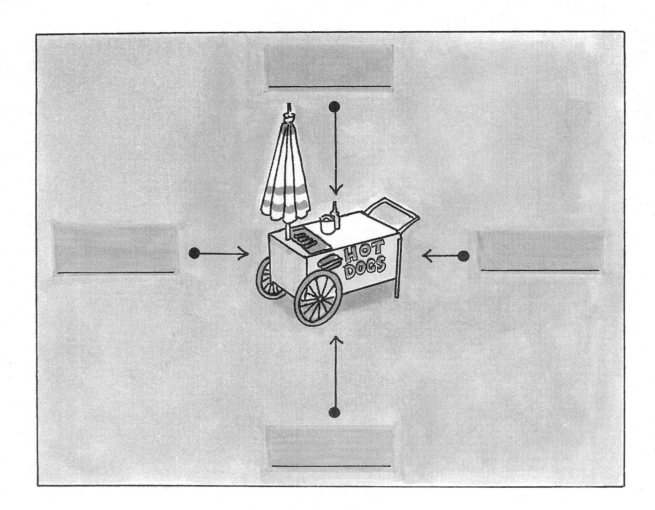

The hot dog stand is south.

Sherlock

The hot dog stand is east.

Molly

The hot dog stand is north.

Bertha

The hot dog stand is west.

Goober

B

The children caught butterflies. They had orange wings.

A

went swimming   stood on a stump   Sherlock   Zelda   painted a picture   Bertha

1.

2.

3.

B

Where is Fred the frog in the afternoon?

a. In the afternoon, all the _____ are on lily pads.

b. Fred is a _____.

c. So in the afternoon, _____.

Ⓐ

| its | gray | scratched | chased | rabbit | ear |

Lesson 45

Goober   Paul   painted a pot   fed the pigs   sat on an apple   Fizz and Liz

1.

2.

3.

C

The girls had pet goats. One of them had very long horns.

Where is Sherlock after dinner?

barn

1. After dinner, all the rats are _____.

2. Sherlock _____.

3. So after dinner, _____.

A

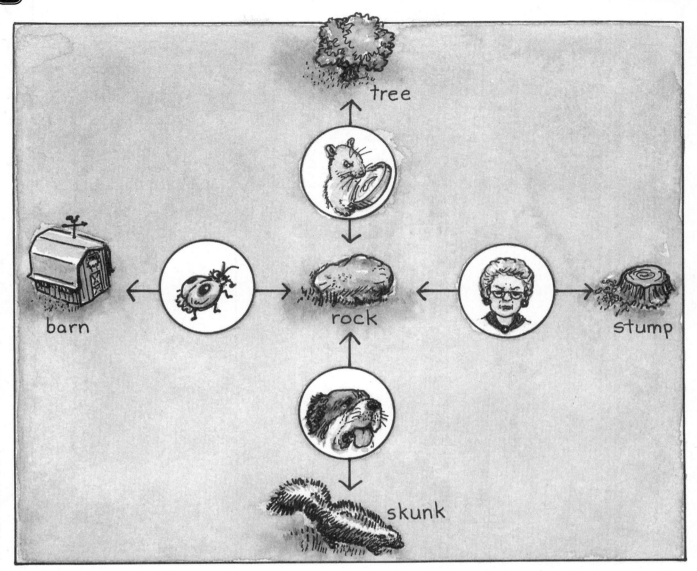

tree

barn

rock

stump

skunk

1. Bertha said, "The rock is _____ of me and the

_____ is _____ of me."

2. Mrs. Hudson said, "The rock is _____ of me and the

_____ is _____ of me."

3. Sherlock said, "The rock is _____ of me and the

_____ is _____ of me."

played in the snow   kissed Bleep   painted a paddle

1.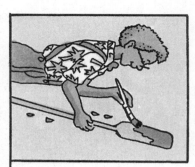

2.

3.

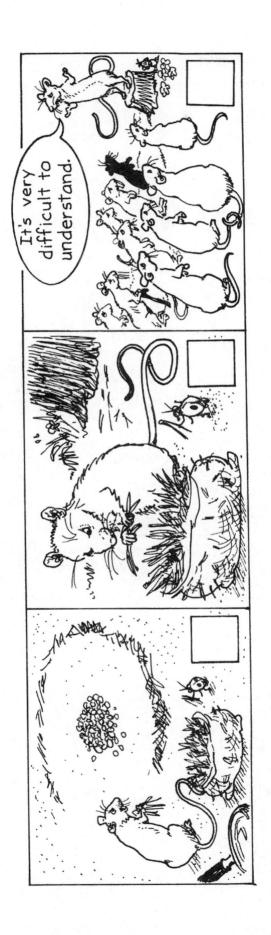

A

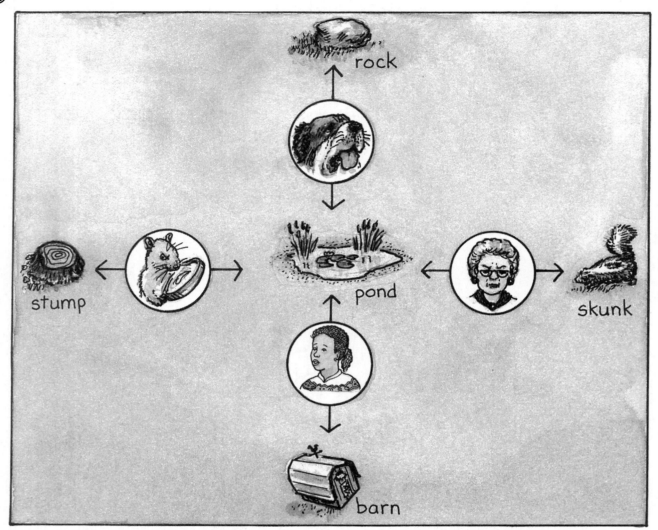

1. Zelda said, "The pond is _____ of me and the

   _____ is _____ of me."

2. Sherlock said, "The pond is _____ of me and the

   _____ is _____ of me."

3. Mrs. Hudson said, "The pond is _____ of me and the

   _____ is _____ of me."

B

played a violin	took a bath	held his hat

1.

2.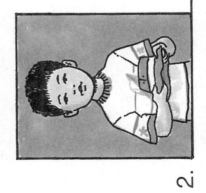

3.

1. The boys played with dogs. The dogs had short tails.

2. The girls went in boats. The boats were made of wood.

3. The truck went up a hill. The truck had a flat tire.

A

| ceiling | short | tall | painting |

Bleep Dud Zelda Mrs. Hudson	rolled in the mud sat on Roger played in the snow chased a skunk said silly things

1. _____

2. _____

3. _____

_____

| ate | spotted | corn | white | goat | grass |

Lesson 50

Test 5

Test Score

A

Molly Bertha Owen Mrs. Hudson	ran home sat on a cake kissed Goober fixed Bleep fed the pigs picked up Owen

1. ______________________________

2. ______________________________

3. ______________________________

Test 5

B

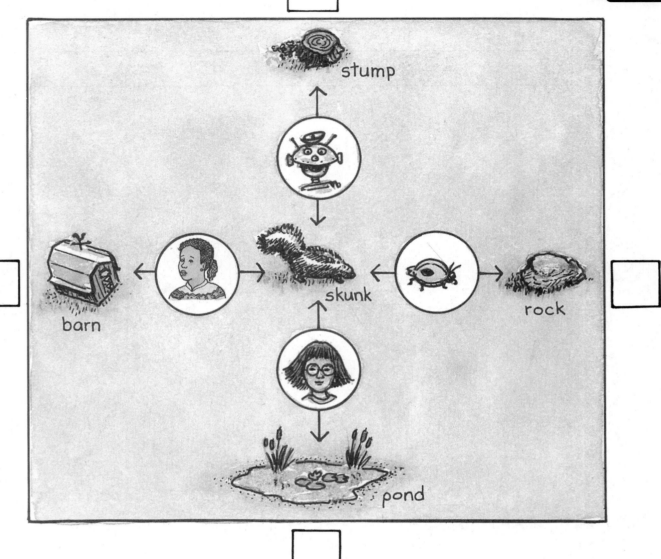

stump

barn

skunk

rock

pond

1. Zelda said, "The skunk is _____ of me and the

   _____ is _____ of me."

2. Molly said, "The skunk is _____ of me and the

   _____ is _____ of me."

3. Bertha said, "The skunk is _____ of me and the

   _____ is _____ of me."

Lesson 50 — Test 5 **149**

young	leaves	chopped	raked

B

1. _____

after he played in the snow.

2. Dud _____

_____.

1. Aunt Martha pulled a turnip out of the dirt.

   The turnip tasted good.

2. The ranger led the dogs toward the mountains.

   The mountains were covered with snow.

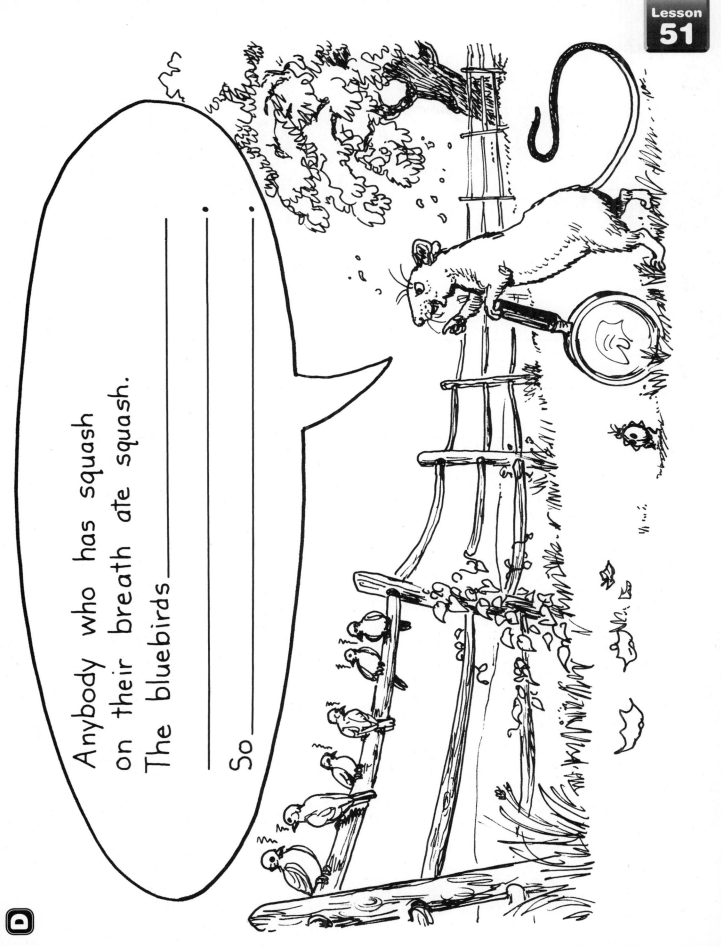

Anybody who has squash
on their breath ate squash.
The bluebirds _____
So _____

A

1. _____

_____

2. _____

_____

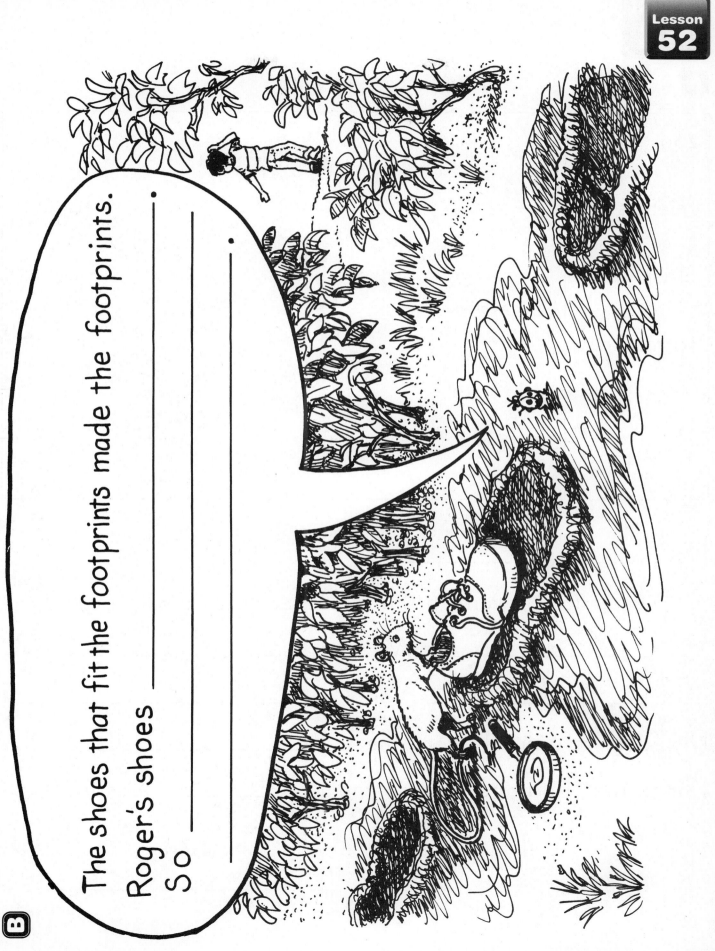

The shoes that fit the footprints made the footprints.

Roger's shoes _____

So _____

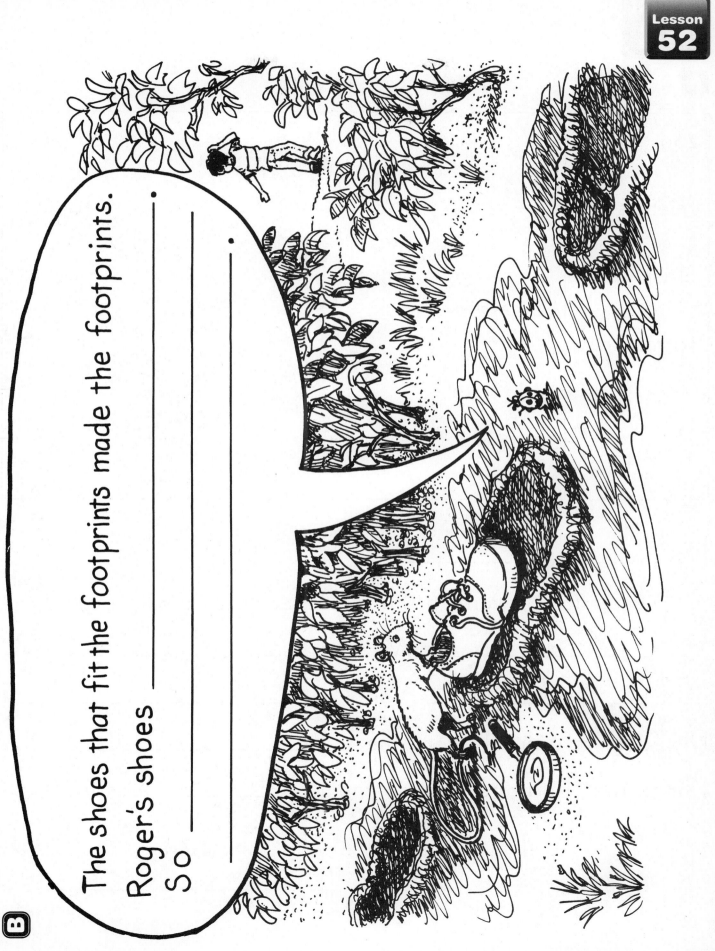

B

A

zoo

friends

class

family

elephants

lions

tigers

bears

monkeys

giraffes

parrots

Dear _____,

    Yesterday, I went to the _____ with my

_____. We saw _____,

_____, and _____.

My favorite animals were the _____.

I hope that I can go back to the _____ soon.

               From,

              _____

B

1. _____

_____

2. _____

_____

The shoes that smell of squash went in squash.

Goober's shoes

So _____

birthday

book

game

paint set

football

kite

play games

eat cake

go swimming

Dear _____ ,

Next week, I will be _____ years old. I am going to

have a _____ party. My friends and I

will _____ and

_____. The birthday present I

want most is a _____. I hope I get it.

From,

_____

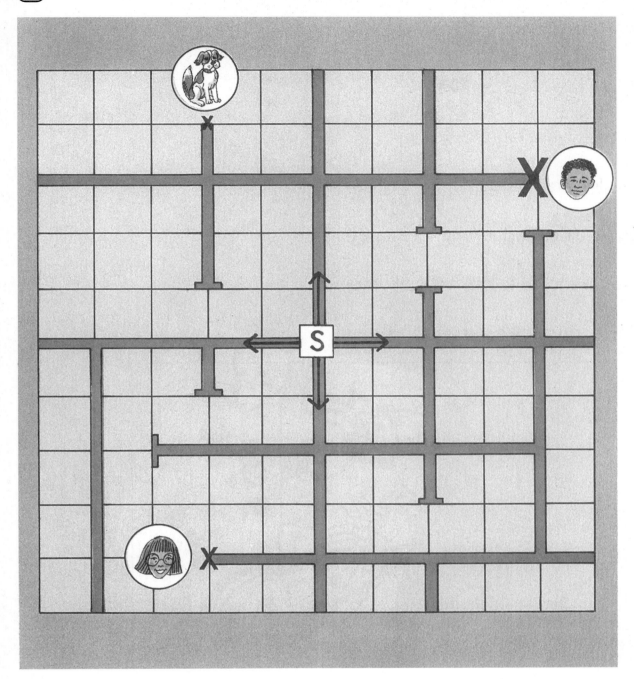

1. To go to Molly, you go _____ miles _____ and _____ miles

   _____.

2. To go to Owen, you go _____ miles _____ and _____ miles

   _____.

1. Three ladies picked berries.

   The berries were blue.

2. Our chicken laid an egg.

   The egg was no bigger than a stone.

3. We used a shovel to plant the flower.

   The flower grew all summer long.

A

school

go for walks

my grandma's

the park

dog

cat

fish

parrot

turtle

hamster

snake

bunny

Dear _____,

    The pet that I would like the most is a _____.

I would name my pet _____, and I would take care

of my _____. We would have a lot of fun together.

I would take my pet to _____ and to _____.

I would love my _____, and my pet would love me.

                         From,

                    _____

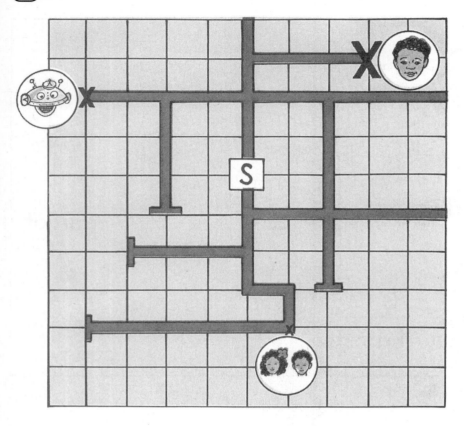

1. To go to Bleep, you go ____ miles _____ and ____ miles

   _____.

2. To go to Owen, you go ____ miles _____ and ____ miles

   _____.

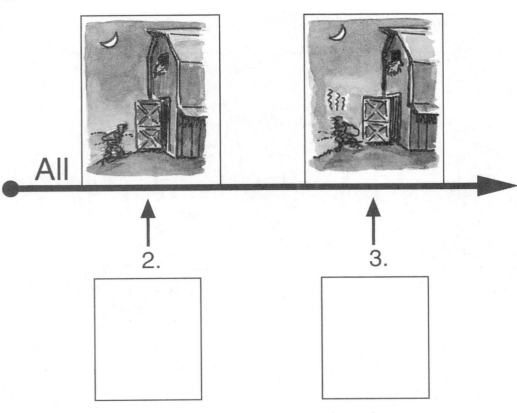

All

2.

3.

a. good   bad

b. good   bad

c. good   bad

D

1. Three little boys picked strawberries. They were as big as apples.

2. Before the children pulled up the tulips, my sister watered them with the hose.

A

1.

2.

3.

1. _____

_____

2. _____

_____

B

1. Zelda drove a van to the picnic. reports does not report

2. Three people sat at a picnic table. reports does not report

3. Everybody was going to swim later that day. reports does not report

4. Roger wore a hat. reports does not report

5. Zelda ate more than anybody else. reports does not report

6. A van was close to the picnic tables. reports does not report

7. Zelda sat next to Mrs. Hudson. reports does not report

C

Donna and her mother watched the tiny spiders. They were upside down in their web.

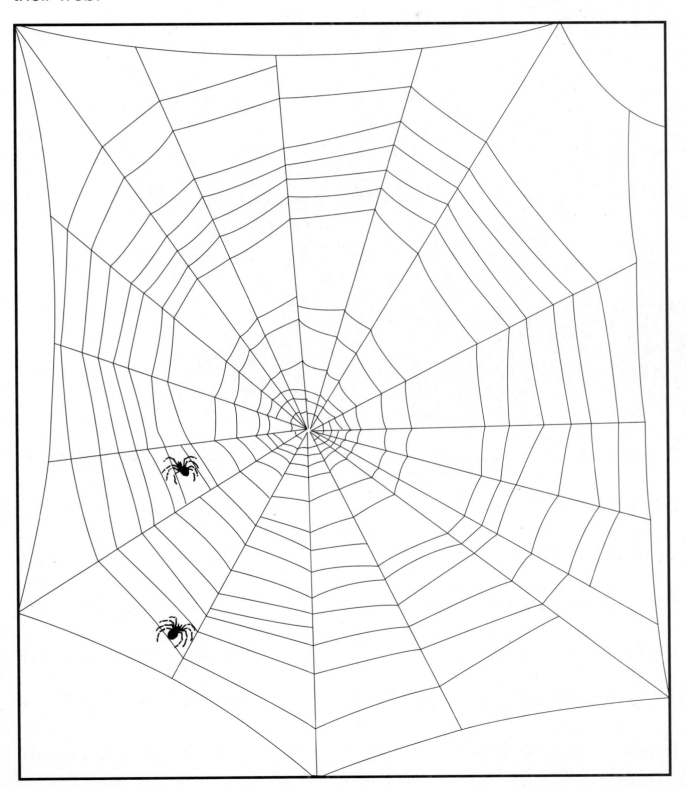

A

1. Sherlock ate too much corn.   reports   does not report

2. Bertha was mad at Sherlock.   reports   does not report

3. Cyrus pulled a large sack.   reports   does not report

4. Bertha played a violin.   reports   does not report

5. The wise old rat was dirty.   reports   does not report

6. The sack was full of hazelnuts.   reports   does not report

7. The wise old rat was wet.   reports   does not report

B

ate a burger
sat under a tree
drove a van
went fishing
ate watermelon
sat on a table
ate pie

C

1. This lamp goes in the bag.

2. I ran on the track.

3. The stamps are in a stack.

D

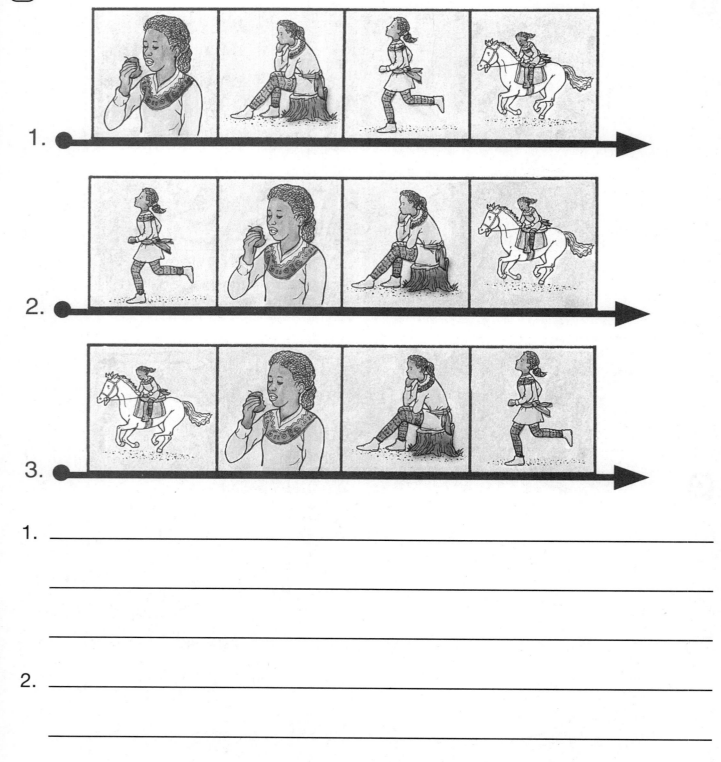

1.

2.

3.

1. _____

_____

_____

2. _____

_____

_____

A

washed	mopped	read	painted
book	window	floor	piano

rode	ate	played	jumped	read
rope	banana	book	violin	bike

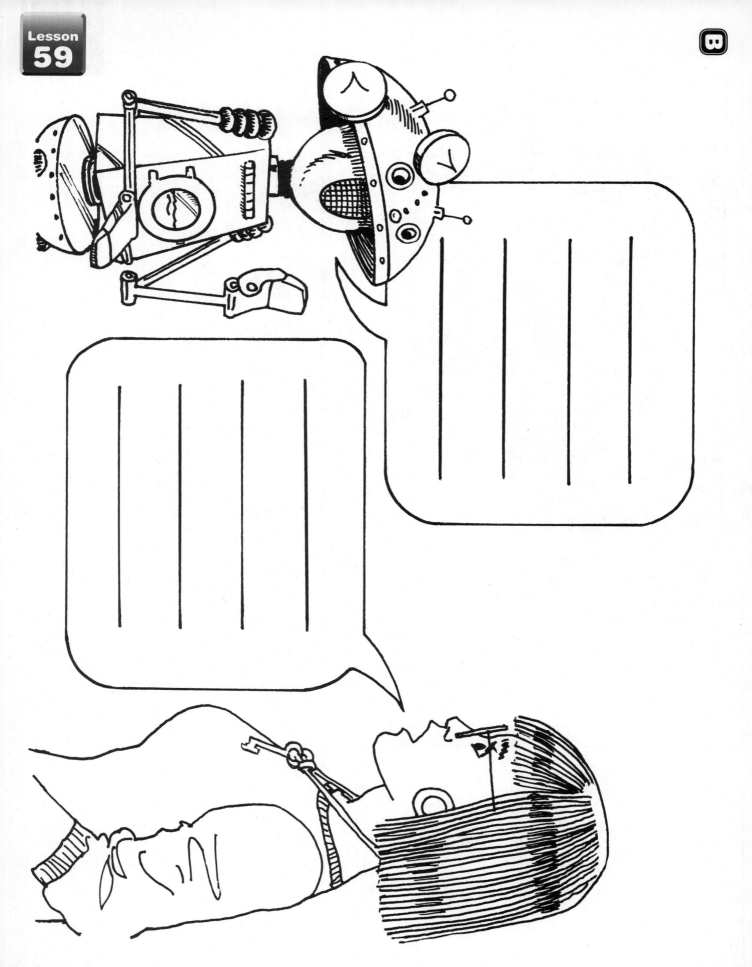

Test 6

Test Score [ ]

A

| striped | bike | rode | patch |
| pants | small | shirt | wore |

Test 6

B

can	cake	corn	rat	tack	bend

C

1. Bleep was holding a can of paint.   reports   does not report

2. Only part of the fence was painted.   reports   does not report

3. Bleep did not hear Molly.   reports   does not report

4. Molly is getting irritated with Bleep.   reports   does not report

5. Molly's car door was open.   reports   does not report

6. Molly called for Bleep's help.   reports   does not report

Ⓐ

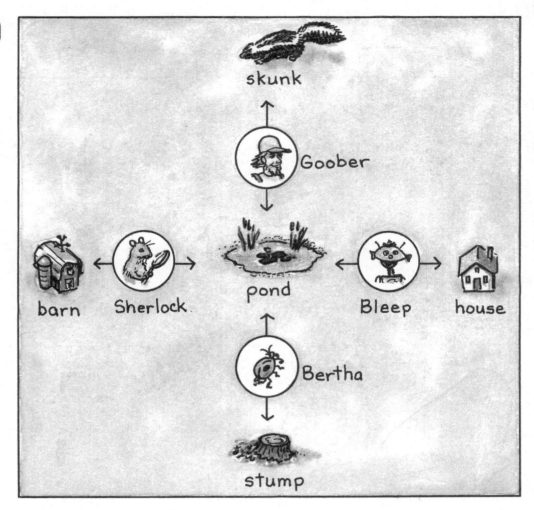

_____ said, "The pond is _____ of me and the

_____ is _____ of me."

_____ said, "The pond is _____ of me and the

_____ is _____ of me."

_____ said, "The pond is _____ of me and the

_____ is _____ of me."

_____ said, "The pond is _____ of me and the

_____ is _____ of me."

| wore | collar | spots | chewed | bone |

It Folds Up

It was regular-sized with two full-sized wheels.

Molly Henderson

Then it folded up to the size of a book.

She said "I got the idea when I talked to him."

Angelo

accordion

A

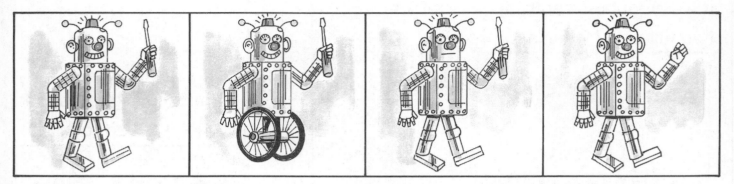

| legs | wheels | smiled | held | screwdriver |

B

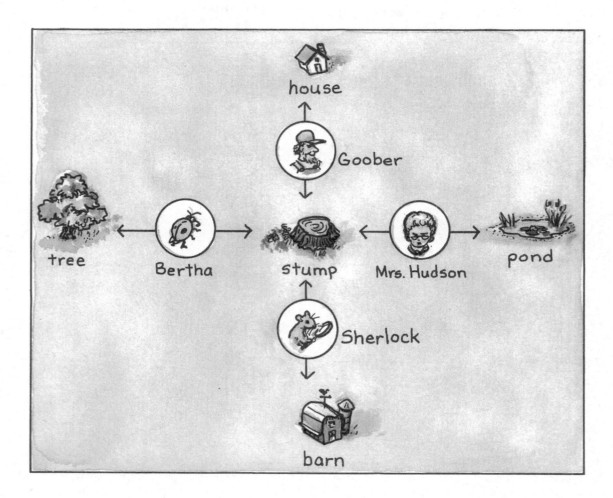

_____ said, "The stump is _____ of me and the

_____ is _____ of me."

_____ said, "The stump is _____ of me and the

_____ is _____ of me."

_____ said, "The stump is _____ of me and the

_____ is _____ of me."

_____ said, "The stump is _____ of me and the

_____ is _____ of me."

C

Map of North America

D

Linda Carry was at it. She was digging in it.

She found them. She sold them.

beach	rooster	gold coins	bushes
trees	ten	sand	turkeys	money

A

1. Mrs. Hudson rode her bike.

2. Mrs. Hudson _____

   _____.

3. Mrs. Hudson _____

   _____.

after	shower	house	took	she

B

| hair | glasses | smiled | long | wore |

C

D

E

1. B is not the safe landing place because B is not

_____

2. C is not the safe landing place because C is not

_____

A

| she | stood | wore | brush |
| chair | hat | used | |

Lesson **64**

B

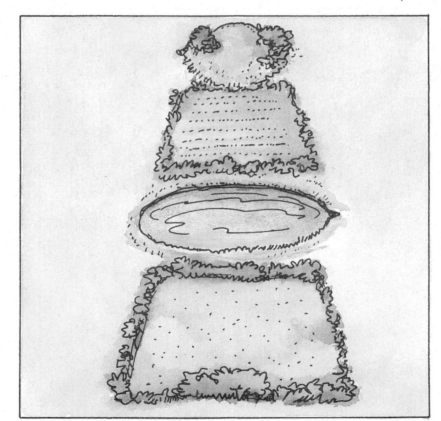

C

apples

pizza

burgers

ice cream

corn on
the cob

macaroni and cheese

read a book

play in the park

draw

_____

Dear _____,

    Here are a few of my favorite things. My favorite things to

eat are _____ and _____. My favorite

things to do are _____ and _____. My

favorite people are _____ and _____.

            From,

            _____

Lesson 64   **191**

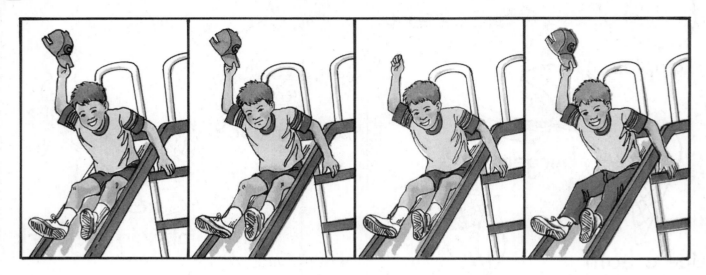

| slid | slide | down | boy | shorts | smiled | held |

C

| three wishes | a vacation a skateboard a magic wand a friend a castle a horse money |

_____

Dear _____,

    This is what I would wish for if I had _____.

First, I would wish for _____. Next, I would wish for

_____. Last, I would wish for _____.

From,

_____

Lesson 62, Part E

A

Circle **reports** if a sentence reports on what the picture shows.
Circle **does not report** if the sentence does not report on what the picture shows.

1. The three men were brothers.	reports does not report
2. Three men fished from a boat.	reports does not report
3. The men were going to have fish for dinner.	reports does not report
4. A big dog stood in the boat.	reports does not report
5. All the men wore hats.	reports does not report
6. One man held a net.	reports does not report
7. One fishing pole bent down toward the water.	reports does not report
8. A large fish was on the end of the line.	reports does not report

B   Circle the part of each sentence that names.

1. The old man went to the store.

2. The man and the boy went to the store.

3. The horse jumped over the fence.

C

Name	
1.	He ate a green apple.
2.	Alice found a dime.
3.	David took a walk in the park.
●	

D

The baby deer   A rabbit   A frog

1.	_____ stood next to the mother deer.
2.	_____ hopped over a log.
3.	_____ sat on a log.

1.	All vehicles can move.
2.	A car is a vehicle.
3.	So _____ .

A

Circle **reports** if a sentence reports on what the picture shows.
Circle **does not report** if the sentence does not report on what the picture shows.

1. The children had been camping for three days.   reports   does not report
2. A girl gave something to a dog.   reports   does not report
3. The girls liked chicken.   reports   does not report
4. Two girls and a boy sat at a picnic table.   reports   does not report
5. Cups and plates were on the table.   reports   does not report
6. The boy petted the dog.   reports   does not report
7. The boy wanted to go home.   reports   does not report

B   Circle the part of each sentence that names.

1. Two girls are eating ice cream.

2. A black cat ran under the fence.

3. A man and a woman sat on the porch.

Lesson 67   **199**

C

● Name	
1.	Alex got a nice gift.
2.	My sister is ten years old.
3.	She fell asleep.
●	

D

1.	_____	held the kite string.
2.	_____	climbed the tree.
3.	_____	was stuck in a tree.

E

1.	All fish have fins.
2.	A bass is a fish.
3.	So _____.

A Circle the part of each sentence that names.

1. A little girl ate two apples.

2. A cow and a horse ate grass.

3. A kite went high in the sky.

4. My brother washed the dishes.

B

A sad clown

A monkey

A bear

Kathy

1.	_____ *rode a bicycle.*
2.	_____ *juggled three balls.*
3.	_____ *walked on the rope.*
4.	_____ *laughed at the clown.*

C

1.	*Every worker uses tools.*
2.	*A plumber is a worker.*
3.	*So _____.*

A   In each blank, write the word that tells what people did.

What people do	What people did
1. burn	
2. fill	
3. push	
4. lick	
5. start	
6. scratch	

B   Put the name of a vehicle in the blanks.

1. All vehicles can move.

2. A _____ is a vehicle.

3. So a _____ can move.

| truck | boat | train | car | plane | bike |

C

1. The little cats were in bed.

2. They were in bed.

3. Five birds sat in the tree.

4. A dog chased a cat.

Lesson 69   **203**

A In each blank, write the word that tells what people did.

What people do	What people did
1. jump	
2. pull	
3. play	
4. push	
5. spill	
6. trick	

B In each blank, write the word that tells what people did.

1. find _found_
2. give _gave_
3. buy _bought_
4. dig _dug_
5. have _had_

6. buy _____
7. find _____
8. dig _____
9. have _____
10. give _____

11. dig _____
12. buy _____
13. have _____
14. give _____
15. find _____

C

1.	Every building has a roof.
2.	A _____ is a building.
3.	So _____ .

a church	a house	a school	a store	a shed

A In each blank, write the word that tells what people did.

1. give *gave*   6. dig _____

2. dig *dug*   7. find _____

3. find *found*   8. buy _____

4. have *had*   9. give _____

5. buy *bought*   10. have _____

B Fix up the sentences so they tell what people did.

1. Alicia <u>was fixing</u> her bike.

2. The girl <u>was talking</u> loudly.

3. Miss Cook <u>is finding</u> her keys.

4. Her grandmother <u>is smiling</u> at the baby.

5. Mr. Howard <u>was buying</u> a picture.

C Circle the part that names. Underline the part that tells more.

1. Three tall girls sat on a horse.

2. They rode the horse across the field.

3. Their horse jumped over a fence.

4. A girl and her horse went across a stream.

5. She rested under a tree.

D

_1._	_Every bird has wings._
_2._	_A _____ is a bird._
_3._	_So _____ ._

a robin	a sparrow	a bluebird	a hawk

A   Circle the part that names. Underline the part that tells more.

1. That sad clown rode on a bicycle.

2. He had a monkey on his head.

3. The monkey went over to Sam.

4. Clowns and monkeys fell down.

5. They made people laugh.

B   Fix up the sentences so they tell what people did.

1. He <u>is giving</u> her a kiss.

2. We <u>were having</u> fun.

3. Boys and girls <u>were buying</u> lunch.

4. The man <u>is painting</u> the house.

5. Josh <u>was finding</u> his socks.

6. Miss Clark <u>is digging</u> in the garden.

C   Fill in the blanks with **He** or **She**.
Remember to start each sentence with a capital.

1. <u>The girl</u> was running.

2. <u>My grandfather</u> read a book.

3. <u>Mary</u> painted the wall.

4. <u>Bill</u> walked home.

5. <u>My brother</u> woke up.

6. <u>His mother</u> washed her hands.

1. _____ was running.

2. _____ read a book.

3. _____ painted the wall.

4. _____ walked home.

5. _____ woke up.

6. _____ washed her hands.

A

1. A boy and his dad went to a baseball game.

2. They ate lots of popcorn.

3. The boy caught a baseball.

4. One baseball player wrote his name on the ball.

5. Yesterday was a wonderful day.

B Fill in the blanks with **He** or **She.**

1. <u>His sister</u> won the race.

2. <u>Her father</u> went to the park.

3. <u>A tall boy</u> washed the car.

4. <u>The young woman</u> fixed the bike.

1. _____ won the race.

2. _____ went to the park.

3. _____ washed the car.

4. _____ fixed the bike.

C Fix up the sentences so they tell what people did.

1. Two children <u>are washing</u> the car.

2. He <u>is spelling</u> a hard word.

3. Wendy <u>is having</u> a party.

4. Nick <u>is buying</u> his sister a hat.

5. He <u>is finding</u> a pencil.

6. She <u>was filling</u> the glass with water.

D

1.	All trees have leaves.
2.	A _____ is a tree.
3.	So _____.

| a maple | a spruce | a pine | a fir | a cedar | a redwood | a birch |

A   Fill in the blanks with **He, She** or **It.**

1. That coat was covered with dirt.   1. _____ was covered with dirt.

2. The rubber ball fell off the table.   2. _____ fell off the table.

3. My mother sat in a chair.   3. _____ sat in a chair.

4. This book was very funny.   4. _____ was very funny.

5. The young woman rode a bike.   5. _____ rode a bike.

6. Susan's game ended early.   6. _____ ended early.

B   Fix up the sentences so they tell what people did.

1. He was having fun.   4. She is buying a dress.

2. She is looking at the sky.   5. Ann is digging in the sand.

3. Alice was picking apples.   6. She was folding the paper.

C   Circle the part that names. Underline the part that tells more.

1. Carla and Tom rode their bikes to the park.

2. They had a picnic with Mary and Beth.

3. A big dog took Tom's sandwich.

4. Rain started to fall.

5. The children went home quickly.

Test 7

A

Alfred

James

Jerry

Circle **reports** if a sentence reports on what the picture shows.
Circle **does not report** if the sentence does not report on what the picture shows.

1.	The cowboys were very hungry.	reports	does not report
2.	Alfred poured soup in a pot.	reports	does not report
3.	James cooked hot dogs over the fire.	reports	does not report
4.	All the cowboys wore hats.	reports	does not report
5.	Jerry used a knife to cut the potato.	reports	does not report
6.	The horse belonged to Jerry.	reports	does not report
7.	The soup smelled good.	reports	does not report
8.	James cooked food over a fire.	reports	does not report

Test 7

B   Next to each word, write the word that tells what people did.

What people do	What people did
1. give	
2. dig	
3. find	
4. save	
5. buy	

C   Circle the part that names. Underline the part that tells more.

1. My brother and my sister were at school.

2. A glass fell off the table.

3. He liked to look at horses.

4. A girl and a boy fixed the fence.

5. They painted the room.

D   Fix up the sentences so they tell what people did.

1. He <u>was giving</u> me a pen.

2. He <u>was buying</u> a shirt.

3. They <u>were picking</u> flowers.

4. He <u>is filling</u> the glass.

5. My friend <u>is having</u> a party.

6. A boy <u>is spelling</u> words.

A In each blank, write the word that tells what people did.

1. wear _wore_

2. see _saw_

3. run _ran_

4. go _went_

5. sit _sat_

6. see _____

7. sit _____

8. go _____

9. wear _____

10. run _____

B Circle the part of each sentence that names.

Tina and Ginger wanted to play in the water. The girls were wearing jeans. They went to the little pool. The two girls went into the shallow water. They started to splash each other. Tina and Ginger were all wet when they left the pool.

C Fill in the blanks with **He, She** or **It.**

1. His big sister parked the car.

2. Ted's car slid down the hill.

3. That movie was interesting.

4. Amanda's brother won the race.

5. The party was fun.

1. _____ parked the car.

2. _____ slid down the hill.

3. _____ was interesting.

4. _____ won the race.

5. _____ was fun.

D Fix up the sentences so they tell what people did.

1. Vanessa is giving the cup to him.

2. Carlos was jumping over a fence.

3. Four children were buying apples.

4. Mr. Lopez was painting a chair.

A Circle the part of each sentence that names.

Carla was in the park. She played on the swings. She went down a slide.

That tired girl rested on a bench. Carla walked home with her friends.

B In each blank, write the word that tells what people did.

1. see _saw_

2. wear _wore_

3. sit _sat_

4. run _ran_

5. go _went_

6. wear _____

7. run _____

8. see _____

9. go _____

10. sit _____

C Fill in the blanks with **He, She** or **It.**

1. His shirt was covered with dirt.

2. My new pencil fell off the table.

3. A boy sat in a chair.

4. Tamika's book was very funny.

5. A young woman rode a bike.

1. _____ was covered with dirt.

2. _____ fell off the table.

3. _____ sat in a chair.

4. _____ was very funny.

5. _____ rode a bike.

D

1.	Every bird has wings.
2.	A _____ is a bird.
3.	So _____ .

| a robin | a crow | a hawk | a chicken |

A Fix up the sentences so they tell what people did.

1. Miss Ross is digging holes for the fence posts.

2. They are filling the box with sand.

3. My grandfather was starting his car.

4. She was having a party.

5. Justin is buying milk.

6. The children were cooking eggs.

B Circle the part of each sentence that names.

An old cowboy rode his horse to town. The cowboy wanted to buy a new hat. He rode his horse to the clothing store. He tied his horse to a post. The cowboy went in the store. He found a hat he liked.

C Fill in the blanks with **He, She** or **It.**

1. That red plate was broken.   1. _____ was broken.

2. Her brother fell down.   2. _____ fell down.

3. My sister had a cold.   3. _____ had a cold.

4. My father's hat was dirty.   4. _____ was dirty.

5. An airplane flew over the clouds. 5. _____ flew over the clouds.

6. Her window was open.   6. _____ was open.

A Fill in the blanks with **He, She** or **It.**

1. Robert spent all morning cleaning his room. _____ put his dirty clothes in the laundry basket.

2. My sister went to the park. _____ played basketball with her friends for two hours.

3. The boat held four people. _____ had three sails.

B Circle the part of each sentence that names.

A little boy found a small box in his yard. The box had three beans in it.

The little boy showed the beans to his sister. She told him to plant the beans.

Three plants grew from the beans. Those plants were made of gold.

C Fix up the sentences so they tell what people did.

1. They were going to the store.

2. He is filling the sink with hot water.

3. My grandmother was fixing her car.

4. She is having fun.

5. Jane was buying a new shirt.

6. A boy is spelling a hard word.

Lesson 80

1. His mother liked to fix cars. _____ worked in a car shop.

2. My father stayed home this morning. _____ read a book.

3. The bus stopped. _____ ran out of gas.

B Fix up the sentences so they tell what people did.

1. Maria wanted a birthday party.

2. She asked some boys and girls to the party.

3. The boys and girls were giving her some presents.

4. Everybody was having fun.

5. The children were playing games outside.

6. They ate cake and ice cream.

C Circle the part of each sentence that names.

Alex taught his pet monkey to do many tricks. The monkey even learned

how to ride a bicycle. Alex dressed his monkey in a costume one day.

Alex and his monkey went to the circus. They showed a clown their

tricks. The clown gave the monkey a job in the circus.

A Fix up the sentences so they tell what people did.

1. They were having fun at the party.
2. Jessica is wearing a new dress.
3. My brother painted his room.
4. Tom and Al are going home.
5. She parked the car.
6. They were starting to run.

B Circle the part of each sentence that names.

Wendy found a dirty old bicycle at the dump. She showed it to her brother. He told his sister that the bicycle was in very poor shape. Wendy worked on the bike every day for a month. It looked like a brand new bike when she was done. She gave it to her brother for his birthday. Wendy and her brother were very happy.

C Fill in the blanks with **He, She** or **It.**

1. Jill went ice-skating. _____ skated with her friends on the pond.

2. Her dad slept on the couch. _____ snored loudly.

3. The motorcycle went by us quickly. _____ made a lot of noise.

4. My kite was new. _____ landed in a tree.

1. Jeff spent two hours doing his homework. _____ worked hard.

2. Jane went to the park. _____ sat and watched the ducks.

3. The cake tasted great. _____ had whipped cream on top.

B Put in capitals and periods. Circle the part of each sentence that names.

A red kite floated into the sky the wind blew the kite three brown ducks

flew near the kite the kite went behind some clouds it went so high that nobody

could see it

C Circle the sentence that tells the main thing each group did.

I.

The cats had long tails.

A cat chewed on a string.

The cats played with string.

The string was on the floor.

2.

The woman cut the grass.

The family was outside.

Everybody wore a hat.

The family worked in the yard.

3.

Three men wore coats and hats.

Three men walked through the snow.

The snow was cold.

The men wore snow shoes.

A Put in capitals and periods. Circle the part of each sentence that names.

A woman rode on a sled six dogs pulled the sled it went through the deep snow the woman was very cold her dogs liked the snow they slept in the snow

B Make each sentence tell what a person or thing did.

Mark looked for a hidden treasure. He is going into his backyard with a shovel. He was digging for a long time. His shovel hit something hard. Mark was reaching into the hole. He pulled something out. He was finding a bone.

Does each sentence tell what a person or thing did? **X X X X**

C Circle the sentence that tells the main thing each group did.

1.

A boy swept the floor.

The room was dirty.

The children cleaned the room.

The children were standing.

2.

All the farmers wore coats.

The farmers fed the animals.

All the farmers were in the barn.

The animals were hungry.

3.

Four girls sat in chairs.

The girls had plates and glasses.

Four girls ate a meal.

The girls sat around the table.

A Circle the part that names. Underline the part that tells more.

1. A horse and a goat were eating grass.

2. Those hungry animals ate all the grass.

3. They drank water from a pond.

4. A car and a truck went by a pond.

5. They were very loud.

B Put in capitals and periods. Circle the part of each sentence that names.

Tom and his brother went shopping for food they bought four apples and

six oranges the food cost less than five dollars Tom gave the clerk five dollars

the clerk gave Tom change

Mr. Walters was buying an apple tree. He dug a hole in his yard. He

placed the tree in the hole. He is filling the hole with dirt. He is watering the

tree. He took good care of the tree.

Do the sentences tell what Mr. Walters did? **X X X**

D Circle the sentence that tells the main thing each group did.

Three cowboys felt tired.

Two cowboys smiled.

The cowboys looked at the fire.

Three cowboys cooked supper.

The animals wore clothing.

The animals did tricks.

The animals were inside.

The animals got food for doing well.

Test 8

Test Score

A Put in capitals and periods. Circle the part of each sentence that names.

My older sister took her dog to the park her dog chased a skunk the skunk got mad it made a terrible stink my sister had to wash her dog for hours to get rid of the smell

B

My friends are going to the park. They are having a good time. Two girls played on the swings. A boy chased a butterfly. A boy and a girl are running in the grass. Everybody is staying in the park until the sun went down.

Do the sentences tell what people did? **X X X X**

Test 8

C Write the letter of each picture that shows what the sentence says.

1. He held a bottle. _____

2. A person held a container. _____

3. She held a container. _____

4. He held a container. _____

D Fill in the blanks with **He, She** or **It.**

1. His shirt was red and blue. _____ had stripes.

2. My mother helped me do my homework. _____ is very good at math.

3. His brother is one year old. _____ can almost walk.

Lesson 85—Test 8   **223**

A Put in capitals and periods. Circle the part of each sentence that names.

Sandy and her dog went for a walk they went to the park a cat ran in front of them the dog started to chase the cat the cat ran up a tree Sandy took her dog home

B Circle the part that names. Underline the part that tells more.

1. My best friend and my sister helped me.

2. She had two dollars.

3. My little sister was sick.

4. The horse fell over.

5. He saw a big bird next to the house.

6. A dog and a cat slept with James.

C In each blank, write the word that tells what somebody did.

1. gets   _got_

2. rides   _rode_

3. drinks   _drank_

4. teaches   _taught_

5. holds   _held_

6. rides   _____

7. teaches   _____

8. gets   _____

9. holds   _____

10. drinks   _____

A   Put in capitals and periods. Circle the part of each sentence that names.

A woman bought a new bike for her son it had big tires the boy liked the

bike his mother showed him how to ride the bike he rode it to school

his teacher let him show the bike to the class

B   Circle the subject. Underline the part that tells more.

1. Three older boys went to the store.

2. A horse and a dog went to a stream.

3. A man sat on a log.

4. They sat on a bench.

5. My friend and his mother were hungry.

6. My hands and my face got dirty.

 C

Mr. Smith and his son are going to the circus. They looked at lions and

tigers. A lion tamer had a whip in his hand. His whip is making a big noise. One

lion is jumping through a hoop. Mr. Smith and his son are having a good time.

Does each sentence tell what someone or something did? **X X X X**

D   In each blank, write the word that tells what people did.

1. rides *rode*

2. holds *held*

3. teaches *taught*

4. drinks *drank*

5. gets *got*

6. teaches _____

7. holds _____

8. gets _____

9. rides _____

10. drinks _____

A Circle the subject of each sentence. Underline the part that tells more.

1. A jet airplane made a lot of noise.

2. A man and his dog went walking.

3. He ate lunch in the office.

4. My brother and his friend played in the park.

5. A little cat drank milk.

B Put in capitals and periods. Circle the subject of each sentence.

Three workers built a dog house a woman nailed boards together she

used a big hammer a young man put a roof on the dog house the workers

finished the dog house in two hours

C In each blank, write the word that tells what somebody did.

1. drinks _____

2. holds _____

3. rides _____

4. gets _____

5. teaches _____

A   Put in the missing capitals and periods.

every student in the class read a book. Tom and Alice read a book about

animals they learned about animals that live in different parts of the world. Two

students read a book about roses that book told how to take care of roses.

B   Circle the subject of each sentence. Underline the predicate.

1. Five cats were on the roof.

2. They read two funny books.

3. A red bird landed on a roof.

4. A dog and a cat played in their yard.

5. It stopped.

C   Fill in the blanks with **He, She** or **It.**

1. My grandmother loves to walk. _____ walks five miles every day.

2. Her brother is ten years old. _____ is in the fifth grade.

3. Our plane will leave at four o'clock. _____ is going to China.

A   Put in the missing capitals and periods.

My class had a picnic everybody went on a bus. Our teacher brought

apples and oranges. He also cooked a chicken we built a fire to cook the

chicken

B   Change the part that names in some of the sentences to **He, She** or **It.**

ⓐSusan loved birds. ⓑSusan wanted to build a bird house.

ⓒHer grandfather gave Susan a book about bird houses.

ⓓHer grandfather told Susan to read it carefully. ⓔThe book was interesting.

ⓕThe book showed how to build a bird house.

C   In each blank, write the word that tells what somebody did.

         1. holds   _____

         2. gets   _____

         3. rides   _____

         4. teaches _____

         5. drinks   _____

A Fix up the paragraph so each sentence begins with a capital and ends with a period.

	A little bird fell out of a tree Bill and his sister saw the little bird. it was in a pile of leaves Bill picked up the little bird his sister climbed up to the nest. Bill handed the bird to his sister she put the bird back in the nest.

B Next to each word, write the word that tells what somebody did.

1. thinks *thought*

2. flies *flew*

3. stands *stood*

4. brings *brought*

5. breaks *broke*

6. stands _____

7. brings _____

8. thinks _____

9. breaks _____

10. flies _____

C Change the part that names in some of the sentences to **He, She** or **It.**

ⓐ The class was playing football during recess. ⓑ Tom had the football.

ⓒ Tom threw the ball as far as he could. ⓓ Alice jumped up and caught the

ball. ⓔ Alice scored a touchdown. ⓕ The school bell rang. ⓖ The school bell

told the class that recess was over.

A   Circle the subject. Underline the predicate.

1. Sara and Rodney painted the kitchen blue.

2. Sara had a paintbrush.

3. Rodney used a roller.

4. They stopped to eat lunch.

5. She laughed.

6. The windows were blue.

B   Next to each word, write the word that tells what somebody did.

1. stands   _stood_

2. thinks   _thought_

3. breaks   _broke_

4. flies   _flew_

5. brings   _brought_

6. breaks _____

7. brings _____

8. flies _____

9. stands _____

10. thinks _____

C   Fix up any sentences in the paragraph that should name **He, She** or **It.**

ⓐ John wanted to have a party for his birthday. ⓑ John was going to be ten years old. ⓒ His mother planned a big party. ⓓ His mother called all John's friends. ⓔ His mother bought lots of party things. ⓕ The party started right after school. ⓖ The party was a lot of fun.

A Fix up the paragraph so each sentence begins with a capital and ends with a period.

Tom threw a rock at a tree his rock hit a beehive. the bees got very mad they flew out of the nest. Tom ran away from the bees. many bees chased him tom jumped into the lake. he never threw rocks at trees again

B Circle the subject. Underline the predicate.

1. Mr. Dunn and his son went to the store.

2. Mrs. Iverson met Mrs. Lopez and her son.

3. Two dogs started to run around the store.

4. Mr. Jones was happy.

5. They sat in a rocking chair.

C Fix up any sentences in the paragraph that should name **He, She** or **It.**

Greg cleaned up his room last week. Greg put all his toys in the closet. His grandmother was very happy. His grandmother gave him a big hug.

D Next to each word, write the word that tells what somebody did.

1. flies _____

2. brings _____

3. breaks _____

4. thinks _____

5. stands _____

E

1.

2.

3.

| white | black | big | small |

1. A _____ cat sat on a _____ chair.

2. A _____ cat sat on a _____ chair.

3. A _____ cat sat on a _____ chair.

A Fix up the paragraph so each sentence begins with a capital and ends with a period.

Snow fell all night long. Doris got up and looked outside everything was white. Doris thought about things to do in the snow she wanted to throw snowballs. She wanted to roll in the snow. her mother handed her a snow shovel. Doris went out in the snow She did not have a lot of fun

B Fix up any sentences in the paragraph that should name **He, She** or **It.**

Sandra wanted to play baseball. Sandra looked for her ball and bat. Her brother also wanted to play baseball. Her brother helped her look for the ball and bat. Sandra looked in the yard. Sandra found the ball and bat near the doghouse. The ball was in bad shape. The ball was all chewed up.

C If a word is somebody's name, begin the word with a capital letter.

nancy	he	truck	tammy	james
they	linda	ann	jack	my	sam
tina	she	window	tim	it

D

1.

2.

3.

beach	tennis

1. _____ woman held a _____ ball.

2. _____ woman held a _____ ball.

3. _____ woman held a _____ ball.

E   Next to each word, write the word that tells what somebody did.

1. stands _____   4. brings _____

2. breaks _____   5. flies _____

3. thinks _____

A

1.

2.

3.

| seat | leg | back | arm |

1. A cat sat on _____ a chair.

2. A cat sat on _____ a chair.

3. A cat sat on _____ a chair.

B

1. Tyrell gets a new dog.

2. His sister teached him to ride a bike.

3. The airplane flied over the mountain.

4. Vanessa standed on a table.

5. We seen an elephant at the circus.

A Circle the subject. Underline the predicate.

1. A young man walked home.

2. It made a big noise.

3. My little sister is sick.

4. Her brother and sister went to school.

5. That pencil belongs to her.

B Fix up the paragraph so each sentence begins with a capital and ends with a period.

a boy threw a rock at a tree the rock missed the tree. The rock hit a

beehive. The bees got mad they chased the boy. he ran all the way home

C Fix up any sentences that should name **He, She** or **It.**

The cooks made pizza. Tom put the pizza in the oven. Tom was very

careful. Jane took the pizza out of the oven. Jane told everybody that they could

eat. The pizza tasted great. The pizza had lots of cheese and tomatoes.

Test 9

D

• An animal sat on a vehicle. • A dog sat on a bike. • An animal sat on a car.

1. Copy the sentence that tells about only one picture.

_____

2. Copy the sentence that tells about two pictures.

_____

3. Copy the sentence that tells about all the pictures.

_____

A   Begin all parts of a person's name with a capital letter.

1. bill jones

2. mrs. williams

3. the doctor

4. his brother

5. anita

6. sam miller

7. this boy

8. mr. adams

9. the girl

10. ted

11. the nurse

12. mrs. cash

B   Fix up the paragraph so each sentence begins with a capital and ends with a period.

a strong wind blew down a tree and a fence a boy and a girl saw the

broken fence the boy got a can of paint the girl got a hammer and nails they

worked very hard to fix the fence

C

1. Lee bringed home a new dog.

2. We thinked about it all night.

3. He standed on the corner.

4. Carlos gots new gloves for his birthday.

5. My mom teached me to ride a bike.

D

| roof | tire | hood | trunk | headlight |

1. A monkey sat on _____ a car.

2. A monkey sat on _____ a car.

3. A monkey sat on _____ a car.

E Circle the subject in each sentence. Underline the predicate.

1. That old house fell down.

2. A new flower came up in the garden.

3. Marcus laughed at the joke.

4. The box was full of money.

5. His room was clean.

6. Three cows and two horses were in the barn.

A Begin all parts of a person's name with a capital letter.

1. mrs. robinson

2. her sister

3. steve crosby

4. a police officer

5. my teacher

6. tigers

7. debbie

8. mr. james

9. a clown

B Fill in the blanks with **He, She, It** or **They.**

1. A man and a woman ate dinner.

2. Two boys walked on the sand.

3. Our bus had a flat tire.

4. Bananas cost 68 cents.

5. The men wore red jackets.

6. That old car went fast.

1. _____ ate dinner.

2. _____ walked on the sand.

3. _____ had a flat tire.

4. _____ cost 68 cents.

5. _____ wore red jackets.

6. _____ went fast.

C   Put in capitals and periods.

a dog ran after a cat the animals ran through the kitchen and the living
room they ran up the stairs and down the stairs the dog ran slower and
slower the cat kept going faster the dog stopped and fell over the cat was
not even tired

D   Rewrite the paragraph so the underlined parts give a clear picture.

An animal fell out of a large old tree. It landed on the soft ground. A
person picked it up. The person put it in a container and took it home.

A Begin all parts of a person's name with a capital letter.

1. greg

2. mrs. abbott

3. my sister

4. cowboys

5. ronnie lee

6. a little poodle

7. jerry adams

8. mr. sanders

9. cats

10. the fireman

11. peggy

12. mrs. jackson

B Fill in the blanks with **He, She, It** or **They.**

1. A cow and a horse drank water.

2. My shoes were wet.

3. Anna played baseball.

4. A boy shouted.

5. His sister stood in line.

6. A bottle fell off the table.

1. _____ drank water.

2. _____ were wet.

3. _____ played baseball.

4. _____ shouted.

5. _____ stood in line.

6. _____ fell off the table.

C

A woman drove an old car she has the car for many years. She took good

care of her car. She even was painting the car. Her car looked as good as new

everybody likes that wonderful old car

☐ **Check 1.** Does each sentence begin with a capital and end with a
period?
☐ **Check 2.** Does each sentence tell what somebody or something did?

D Write **S** in front of each part that is a subject.
Write **P** in front of each part that is a predicate.

_____ 1. ran to the store

_____ 2. had a long tail

_____ 3. my dog

_____ 4. Troy and Chris

_____ 5. had four new tires

_____ 6. she

_____ 7. my sister

_____ 8. was on the table

_____ 9. two dogs and three cats

_____ 10. bought a yellow dress

E

1. He breaked his leg.

2. They rided a horse.

3. I seen my brother in the park.

4. Tamika gots an A on the test.

5. Tyrell drinked a glass of water.

F Rewrite the paragraph so the underlined parts give a clear picture.

A <u>man</u> sat on <u>an object</u>. A <u>bird</u> sat on <u>him</u>. He held <u>it</u> in one hand. He tossed <u>food</u> with the other hand. Three <u>animals</u> picked up the <u>food</u>.

Lesson 99

A Write **S** in front of each part that is a subject.
Write **P** in front of each part that is a predicate.

_____ 1. Jerry and Tom

_____ 2. walked to the store

_____ 3. played cards with Jill

_____ 4. my brother and I

_____ 5. three eggs

_____ 6. went to the movies

_____ 7. they

_____ 8. she

_____ 9. talked to the doctor

_____ 10. had fun with his friend

B

A car went past our house. It has old tires it had four broken doors. The

car was making lots of noise smoke came out of the hood. The driver is getting

out of the car he is kicking the car his car fell apart.

☐ **Check 1.** Does each sentence begin with a capital and end with a
period?
☐ **Check 2.** Does each sentence tell what somebody or something did?

C   Fill in the blanks with **He, She, It** or **They.**

1. Two women fixed the car.   1. _____ fixed the car.

2. My father bought a new tie.   2. _____ bought a new tie.

3. The boys and girls played baseball.   3. _____ played baseball.

4. Jill found ten dollars.   4. _____ found ten dollars.

5. His bag was full of apples.   5. _____ was full of apples.

6. Those apples were not ripe.   6. _____ were not ripe.

7. Her sisters fixed Jim's car.   7. _____ fixed Jim's car.

8. David fed the dog.   8. _____ fed the dog.

D   Begin all parts of a person's name with a capital letter.

1. alice   5. the new boss   9. a fire fighter

2. mr. martinez   6. robert   10. sally

3. my brother   7. mrs. adams   11. carl sanders

4. the doctor   8. a big fish   12. that teacher

E   Rewrite the paragraph so the underlined parts give a clear picture.

A man was carrying some food. He saw some animals. He dropped it and climbed up a plant. Some of the animals ate it. Some of the animals looked up at the man.

James had two good friends. Their names were jill adams and robert gomez. jill and robert went to the same school that james went to. Their teacher was mr. ray.

☐ **Check.** Does each part of a person's name begin with a capital? **(9)**

B Cross out some of the names and write **He, She, It** or **They.**

Tom and Mary went to the airport. Tom and Mary were going to meet their dad in San Francisco. Tom had never been on a plane before. Tom was very frightened. Tom and Mary sat together on the plane. Tom and Mary had fun after Tom stopped worrying.

C In each blank, write the word that tells what somebody did.

1. swims   *swam*
2. begins   *began*
3. comes   *came*
4. draws   *drew*
5. takes   *took*

6. draws   _____
7. takes   _____
8. begins   _____
9. comes   _____
10. swims   _____

D Write **S** in front of each part that is a subject.
Write **P** in front of each part that is a predicate.

_____ 1. went to the circus

_____ 2. our family

_____ 3. laughed at the clowns

_____ 4. was very exciting

_____ 5. lions and tigers

_____ 6. my sister

_____ 7. sat under a large tree

_____ 8. Tom and his sister

_____ 9. ate dinner with us

_____ 10. they

E Rewrite the paragraph so the underlined parts give a clear picture.

She was riding a vehicle. She was in the middle of it. An animal jumped in front of it. She turned sharply. The vehicle ran into a plant. The plant damaged it.

A Fix up the paragraph so that none of the sentences begin with **and** or **and then.**

Morgan threw a Frisbee to his dad. And it went over his dad's head.

And then his dad ran after the Frisbee. And then he tripped in the mud.

Morgan started to run after the Frisbee. And a big dog picked it up before

Morgan could grab it. And then the dog ran away with it. And then Morgan

chased after the dog. His dad went in the house to clean up.

B

1. draws *drew*

2. swims *swam*

3. begins *began*

4. takes *took*

5. comes *came*

6. begins _____

7. comes _____

8. draws _____

9. swims _____

10. takes _____

C

They cleaned the animal. She wore great big shoes and dark

glasses. She squirted the animal with a hose. He wore a cowboy

hat. He sat on the animal and scrubbed its back. She wore a funny

suit and a tiny hat. She stood on a ladder. She poured it on the

animal.

A

We had a good time at the park Tom played basketball with bob. Alice

and jane went jogging. I listened to mr. anderson read from a book my sister

went swimming we got home just in time for dinner

☐ **Check 1.** Does each sentence begin with a capital and end with a
period?
☐ **Check 2.** Does each part of a person's name begin with a capital letter?

B

Sandra went to the zoo yesterday. And then she met her friends near the

monkey house. And the monkeys were doing tricks. Two monkeys were

swinging by their tails. And one monkey was doing flips. And then Sandra and

her friends went to the snack bar. And they bought peanuts for the monkeys.

C

They were in a corral. It drove up. It started to make a loud

noise. They were in it. He grabbed a rope and jumped out of it.

They stayed in it.

Lesson
103

Circle the subject. Underline the predicate.

1. Carlos built a fire.

2. Susan and Vanessa are planning a party.

3. My old clock was broken.

4. It is very cold.

5. The horses and cows stood in the barn.

6. They gave a prize to every child.

Ⓑ

Everybody went to the beach. And Jerry and alice built a fire on the

sand. And then Tom and bill roasted hot dogs and marshmallows. And Mr.

jones and sammy played ball.

☐ **Check 1.** Did you fix each sentence that started with **and** or **and then?**
☐ **Check 2.** Does each part of a person's name begin with a capital letter?

Ⓒ Write the word that tells what somebody did.

1. comes _____   4. takes _____

2. swims _____   5. begins _____

3. draws _____   6. thinks _____

A

Sam and Ellen are cooking supper for their family. Ellen made hamburgers she cooked them over a fire. Sam makes corn he was putting butter and salt on each piece. Everyone likes the meal.

☐ **Check 1.** Does each sentence begin with a capital and end with a period?

☐ **Check 2.** Does each sentence tell what somebody or something did?

B   Fix up the run-on sentences.

1. Two girls played football and their dad watched them and then they asked him if he wanted to play.

2. A boy asked his mother for some food and then she gave him an apple and he asked if he could also have some cheese and his mother gave him a piece of cheese.

C

They came out of the building.   They walked toward it.

She carried it.   He carried them.   She waved to them.

 A   Fix up the run-on sentences.

1. Mr. Clark went for a ride in the country and then his car ran out of gas and

    then he had to walk three miles to a gas station.

2. Kathy likes to read books and her favorite book was about horses and her

    brother gave her that book.

3. Pam's mother asked Pam to mow the lawn and then Pam started to cut

    the grass and it was too wet.

Test 10

Test Score

A   Fix up each person's name so all parts of the name begin with a
capital.

1. nancy jackson   6. her brother

2. mrs. williams   7. mrs. nelson

3. my father   8. an old man

4. mr. adams   9. david jordan

5. robert smith

Test 10

B Fill in the blanks with **He, She, It** or **They.**

1. Two girls ate lunch.

2. A cow and a horse slept in the barn.

3. His sister went home.

4. The blue pen fell off the desk.

5. James is sick today.

6. My friends went to a party.

1. _____ ate lunch.

2. _____ slept in the barn.

3. _____ went home.

4. _____ fell off the desk.

5. _____ is sick today.

6. _____ went to a party.

C Circle the subject. Underline the predicate.

1. My little sister had fun at school.

2. They were sleeping.

3. A man and a woman walked in the park.

4. Her friend won the race.

5. She stopped working at noon.

6. My green pen cost two dollars.

A   Fill in the blanks with the correct words.

Three women worked on a house.

_____ wore work clothes.

_____ cut a board. _____

used a saw. _____ carried three

pieces of wood. _____ carried the

boards on her shoulder. _____ hammered nails into the wood.

Kay   Milly   Jean

B   Fix up the run-on sentences.

1. Miss Wilson saw a used bike at a store and the bike was red and blue and
   then Miss Wilson bought it for her sister. (3)

2. Richard and his sister went to a movie and it was very funny and Richard
   and his sister ate popcorn and then their mother picked them up after the
   movie. (4)

3. Tina built a doghouse for her dog and then she looked in the doghouse
   and four cats were in the doghouse with her dog. (3)

C

1. Six bottles were on the table.

2. An old lion chased the rabbit.

3. Jane and Sue sat under a tree.

4. His brother had a candy bar.

D

A woman lived near our school Her name was mrs. jones she was an

airplane pilot. She told us many stories about flying planes

☐ **Check 1.** Does each sentence begin with a capital and end with a
period?
☐ **Check 2.** Does each part of a person's name begin with a capital letter?

1. A black pencil fell off the table.

2. My sister was sick.

3. A dog and a cat played in the park.

4. They smiled.

5. Ana sang softly.

6. An old horse drank from a bucket.

B Fix up the run-on sentences in this paragraph.

Don found a lost dog and the dog had a collar around its neck. The
collar had a phone number on it and then Don called the phone number
and the dog's owner answered the telephone. The owner was happy that Don
found the dog. He went to Don's house and then Don gave the dog to the
owner.

C For each verb that tells what somebody does, write the verb that tells
what somebody did.

1. begins _____

2. brings _____

3. flies _____

4. swims _____

5. takes _____

6. comes _____

D Fill in the blanks with the correct words.

_____ sat in the

wheelchair. _____ wore pajamas.

The _____ had big wheels and

little wheels. _____ had a seat, a

back and two handles. _____ held

a purse. _____ wore a skirt and

a sweater. _____ was behind the

wheelchair. _____ pushed the wheelchair.

Ruth   Dora

Ben

wheelchair

1. She jumped into the pool.

2. A young woman read a book about dinosaurs.

3. My mother had a new car.

4. They laughed.

5. My brother and my sister ate cookies and ice cream.

B

Serena went on an airplane and she had never been on an airplane before. She sat in a seat next to the window and the plane took off. She fell asleep for an hour and she woke up and the plane landed. Her grandmother was waiting for her.

C Fill in the blanks with the correct words.

_____ and _____ worked in the garden. _____ wore work clothes. _____ dug a hole. _____ pushed the shovel down with her foot. _____ sawed a branch. _____ held the branch with one hand.

James

Alice

A   Fix up the run-on sentences in the paragraph.

Jessica and Mark bought a pumpkin for Halloween and the pumpkin was so big that they could not carry it home. They started to roll it home. They pushed the pumpkin up a steep hill and then Mark slipped. The pumpkin rolled down the hill. It smashed into a tree and Jessica and Mark had lots of pumpkin pie the next day.

B

1. walked   2. smiled   3. picked   4. cried

was walking      

C   Write the missing word in each item.

1. the hat that belongs to the boy   the ____*boy's*____ hat

2. the bone that belongs to the dog   the _____ bone

3. the car that belongs to her father   her _____ car

4. the arm that belongs to the girl   the _____ arm

5. the book that belongs to my friend   my _____ book

6. the toy that belongs to the cat   the _____ toy

A Fix up the run-on sentences in the paragraph.

Ronald put his finger in a bottle and his finger got stuck in the bottle and then he asked his sister to help him. His sister got some butter and then she rubbed the butter around the top of the bottle. She pulled on the bottle and then his finger came out.

B Circle the subject. Underline the predicate. Make a **V** above every verb.

1. The boy walked to the store.

   The boy was walking to the store.

2. Two girls ate candy.

   Two girls were eating candy.

3. A fish swam in the bathtub.

   A fish was swimming in the bathtub.

C

1. the dress that belongs to the girl   the ___*girl's*___ dress

2. the tent that belongs to her friend   her _____ tent

3. the toy that belongs to my cat   my _____ toy

4. the watch that belongs to that boy   that _____ watch

5. the hammer that belongs to his mother   his _____ hammer

6. the leg that belongs to my father   my _____ leg

Additional Practice
Test 7

A   Circle the part that names. Underline the part that tells more.

1. They ate lunch in the park.

2. We saw three monkeys at the zoo.

3. A lion and a tiger were sleeping.

4. An old woman sat in front of me.

5. My brother and my sister were at school.

6. Their little dog barked all night.

B   Circle the part that names. Underline the part that tells more.

1. My shirt and my pants were dirty.

2. A big truck went up the hill.

3. She fixed the broken window.

4. A man and a woman were in the car.

5. He walked to school.

6. Six red ants climbed onto the table.

Fix up the sentences so they tell what people did.

1. She is buying a shirt.

2. My teacher was giving me a book.

3. The dog is licking my face.

4. Her mother is finding the keys.

5. She was walking quickly.

6. They are spilling the water.

Fix up the sentences so they tell what people did.

1. Robin is starting her car.

2. Our class was having a party.

3. James is digging in the sand.

4. They were pushing the car.

5. Mr. Adams is finding his keys.

6. Alice was filling the glass.

Additional Practice

Test 8

A

Put in capitals and periods.
Circle the part of each sentence that names.

mr. James cooked an apple pie he put the pie on the kitchen table a fly flew into the kitchen it landed on the apple pie mr. James got mad he swung a flyswatter at the fly he missed the fly he hit the pie the pie splattered all over the kitchen

B

Put in capitals and periods.
Circle the part of each sentence that names.

a little boy threw a ball the ball rolled into the street a big truck ran over the ball the boy started to cry the truck driver got out of the truck he bought a new ball for the boy

C

Robin and her little sister are going to the swimming pool. They are wearing their new bathing suits. They stayed at the pool all day. Robin is sitting in the sun. Her little sister is playing in the water.

Do the sentences tell what people did? **X X X X**

D

James is having a bad cold. He stayed home from school. He is wearing pajamas all day. He is sitting in front of the bedroom window. His mother is giving him hot soup.

Do the sentences tell what people did? **X X X X**

E   Fill in the blanks with **He, She** or **It.**

1. My father went swimming. _____ wore his new bathing suit.

2. His bike could go very fast. _____ had big tires.

3. My sister is eleven years old. _____ is in fifth grade.

F   Fill in the blanks with **He, She** or **It.**

1. Her brother was tired. _____ did not get enough sleep.

2. My grandmother called us. _____ asked us about school.

3. Her house is very big. _____ has four bedrooms.

Test 9

A   Circle the subject. Underline the predicate.

1. My sister was tired.

2. We tried to find it.

3. They flew away.

4. That little cat slept under the bed.

5. My teacher and his wife live near the school.

6. We saw Mr. Adams and his son.

B   Circle the subject. Underline the predicate.

1. They sat in a big old chair.

2. It stopped.

3. My red pencil fell off the table.

4. A cat and a dog chased the skunk.

5. Five striped cats played under the house.

6. A boy slept on the couch.

C   Fix up the paragraph so each sentence begins with a capital and ends with a period.

A truck went up the hill. The truck went over a rock a big barrel fell out of the truck. the barrel rolled down the hill it crashed into a tree the barrel broke into little pieces.

Additional Practice   **267**

Fix up the paragraph so each sentence begins with a capital and ends with a period.

Bill's dog chased a butterfly. the butterfly flew away the dog ran through a big mud puddle. Bill took the dog into the bathroom he gave the dog a bath. the dog was not happy She wanted to play

Fix up any sentences that should name **He, She** or **It.**

The children made a big sand castle at the beach. Robert made the walls. Robert used sand that was very wet. His sister made the towers. His sister worked very carefully. The sand castle was three feet high. The sand castle looked like something you would see in a book.

Fix up any sentences that should name **He, She** or **It.**

Linda had a birthday yesterday. Linda was eleven years old. Her father brought a cake to school. Her father gave cake to each student. The cake tasted great. The cake had chocolate and strawberry filling.

Additional Practice

Test 10

A Fix up each person's name so all parts of the name begin with a capital.

1. alan davis

2. mr. james

3. my teacher

4. a doctor

5. robert crosby

6. her sister

7. david tanaka

8. my best friend

9. david jackson

B Fix up each person's name so all parts of the name begin with a capital.

1. mrs. jackson

2. two cowboys

3. paul adams

4. ronnie nolasco

5. my sister

6. that fire fighter

7. mrs. ray

8. michael walker

9. a football player

C　Fill in the blanks with **He, She** or **They.**

1. Her friends went home.　　　1. _____ went home.

2. A dog and a cat chased the skunk. 2. _____ chased the skunk.

3. Her brother came home early.　3. _____ came home early.

4. His toy was broken.　　　　　4. _____ was broken.

5. My sister drove the car.　　　5. _____ drove the car.

6. The girls helped me.　　　　6. _____ helped me.

D　Fill in the blanks with **He, She** or **They.**

1. That old truck went fast.　　1. _____ went fast.

2. Apples cost 42 cents.　　　　2. _____ cost 42 cents.

3. The men wore cowboy hats.　3. _____ wore cowboy hats.

4. His mother talked on the phone. 4. _____ talked on the phone.

5. Our car had a flat tire.　　　5. _____ had a flat tire.

6. Her friends went home.　　　6. _____ went home.

E Circle the subject. Underline the predicate.

1. Three horses and a cow were in the barn.

2. She fell asleep.

3. A little bird flew into the house.

4. It was very large.

5. A big glass was next to the plate.

6. They stopped suddenly.

F Circle the subject. Underline the predicate.

1. His dad went into the house.

2. He talked.

3. Two girls and a boy entered the room.

4. That friendly animal smiled at us.

5. It stopped.

6. Everybody started to talk.

Story words

a rock	a fish	a hat	a farm	a hound	berries
a dress	a bottle	a goat	Mrs. Hudson	Fizz and Liz	Clarabelle
a coat	Zelda	a house	a plum	ice cream	a frog
Dot	a bone	a stick	a hot dog	Owen	nuts
a picture	a note	a violin	Goober	a snake	a worm
a ladder	money	Dud	a tree	a bug	a tub
an apple	a toad	a town	a hamburger	a duck	Sweetie
a shoe	an elephant	a pie	a pizza	a boat	a bird

Lesson 27	Lesson 24
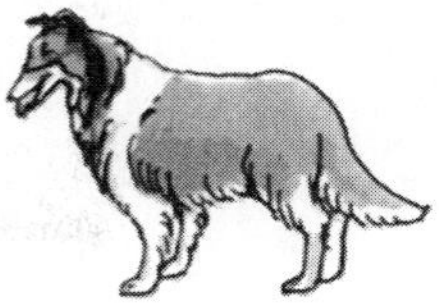 Collie	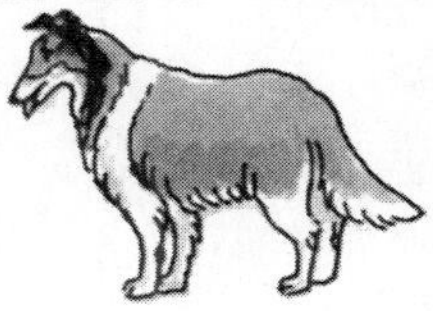 Collie
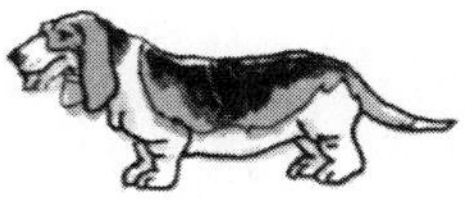 Basset	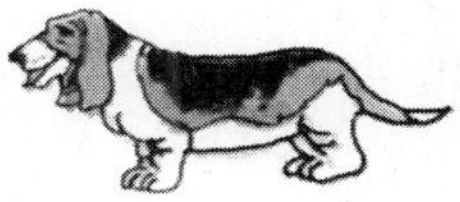 Basset
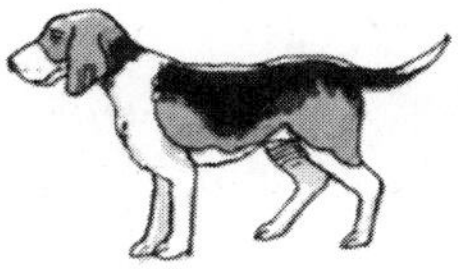 Beagle	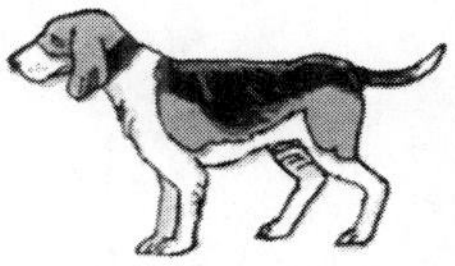 Beagle
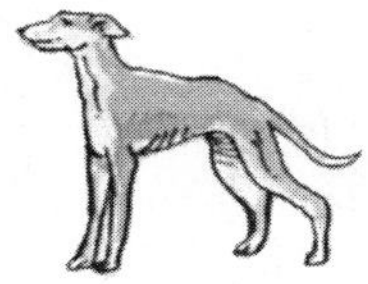 Greyhound	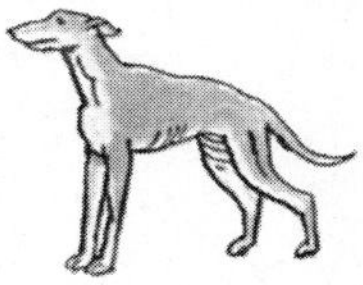 Greyhound
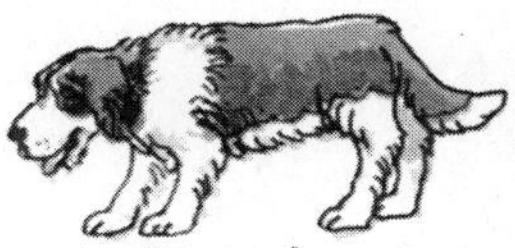 Saint Bernard	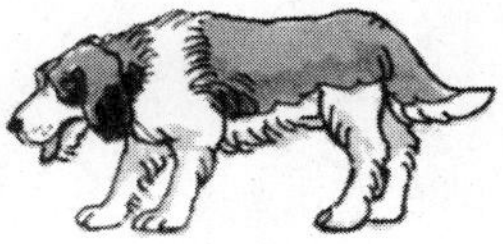 Saint Bernard
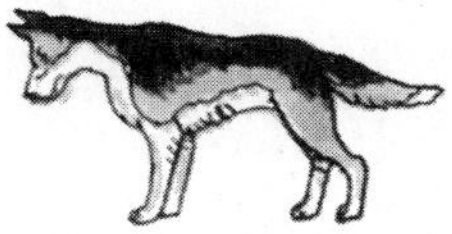 German shepherd	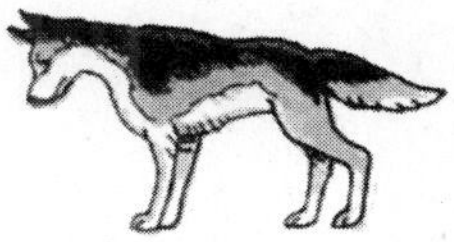 German shepherd
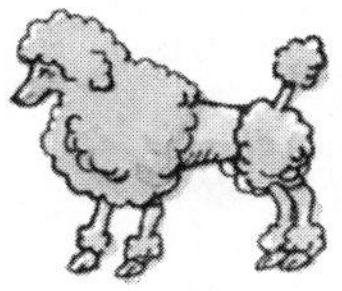 Poodle	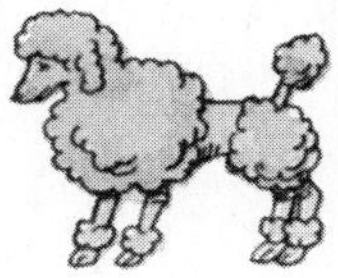 Poodle
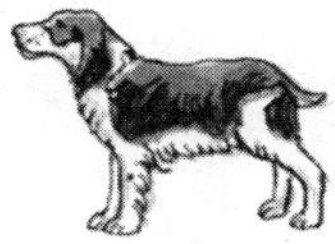 Springer spaniel	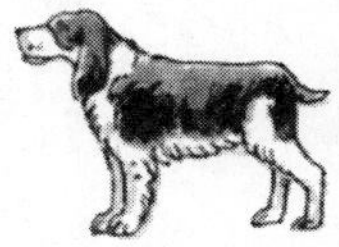 Springer spaniel